How to Direct Shakespeare

RELATED TITLES

Directing Shakespeare in America: Current Practices
Charles Ney
978-1-4742-3983-7

Staging Shakespeare: A Director's Guide to Preparing a Production
Brian Kulick
978-1-3502-0102-6

Shakespearean Tragedy
Kiernan Ryan
978-1-4725-8698-8

How to Direct Shakespeare

Adrian Noble

THE ARDEN SHAKESPEARE
LONDON • NEW YORK • OXFORD • NEW DELHI • SYDNEY

THE ARDEN SHAKESPEARE
Bloomsbury Publishing Plc
50 Bedford Square, London, WC1B 3DP, UK
1385 Broadway, New York, NY 10018, USA
29 Earlsfort Terrace, Dublin 2, Ireland

BLOOMSBURY, THE ARDEN SHAKESPEARE and the Arden Shakespeare logo are trademarks of Bloomsbury Publishing Plc

First published in Great Britain 2022

Copyright © Adrian Noble, 2022

Adrian Noble has asserted his right under the Copyright, Designs and Patents Act, 1988, to be identified as the author of this work.

For legal purposes the Acknowledgements on pp. xii-xiii constitute an extension of this copyright page.

Cover design by Tjaša KrivecBarry Lynch (Puck, right) with a fairy in A Midsummer Night's Dream by Shakespeare at the Royal Shakespeare Company (RSC), 03/08/1994. Design: Anthony Ward, lighting: Chris Parry, director: Adrian Noble. © Donald Cooper/Photostage

All rights reserved. No part of this publication may be reproduced or transmitted in any form or by any means, electronic or mechanical, including photocopying, recording, or any information storage or retrieval system, without prior permission in writing from the publishers.

Bloomsbury Publishing Plc does not have any control over, or responsibility for, any third-party websites referred to or in this book. All internet addresses given in this book were correct at the time of going to press. The author and publisher regret any inconvenience caused if addresses have changed or sites have ceased to exist, but can accept no responsibility for any such changes.

A catalogue record for this book is available from the British Library.

Library of Congress Cataloging-in-Publication Data
Names: Noble, Adrian, 1950- author.
Title: How to direct Shakespeare / Adrian Noble.
Description: London; New York: The Arden Shakespeare, 2022. | Includes index.
Identifiers: LCCN 2022004196 | ISBN 9781350231245 (hardback) | ISBN 9781350231238 (paperback) | ISBN 9781350231269 (ebook) | ISBN 9781350231252 (epub) | ISBN 9781350231276
Subjects: LCSH: Shakespeare, William, 1564–1616–Dramatic production–Handbooks, manuals, etc. | Theater–Production and direction.
Classification: LCC PR3091 .N629 2022 | DDC 792.02/33–dc23/eng/20220406
LC record available at https://lccn.loc.gov/2022004196

ISBN:	HB:	978-1-3502-3124-5
	PB:	978-1-3502-3123-8
	ePDF:	978-1-3502-3126-9
	eBook:	978-1-3502-3125-2

Typeset by Integra Software Services Pvt. Ltd.

To find out more about our authors and books visit www.bloomsbury.com and sign up for our newsletters.

For Joanne, Rose and Jude, my companions in lockdown

Contents

List of Figures xi
Acknowledgements and Thanks xii

Introduction 1

1 You 9

2 Him 13

3 The Director and the Text 17
    Part One: The World (Who's Who) 17
    Part Two: Reading the Play 24
    Part Three: Analysing the Play 26
    Part Four: Entering Shakespeare's World 31

4 Awayday 1: Dramatic Energy (How Does He Do It?) 45
    Apposition 46
    Metaphor 50
    Metre and Pulse 53
    Line Endings 56
    Word Play: Rhyme, Alliteration and Assonance 59
    Vocabulary 61
    Shape and Structure 64

5 Let's Design It! The Eye 69
   Your Designer 69
   To Start: 71
     Wall of ideas 71
     Read out loud 72
     Analyse and discuss 72
     Brainstorm 73
   The Model 74
   A Methodology 75
     Space 75
     The mechanics: Floors 77
     The mechanics: Entrances and exits 78
     The mechanics: Axes 80
     The mechanics: Walls 82
     The Skeleton 83
   The Journey of the Play: Two Casebooks 84
   Playtime 86
   'In the Round' 90
   Thrust Stages 92
   Technology of Design: How to Get from A to B 94
   Colour, Texture and Decoration 95
   Storyboard 97
   Show and Tell 97
   FAQ: Design 98
     What if they don't like what we've done? 98
     What if my designer and I get stuck? 99
     What if someone asks 'What is your concept?' 99
     When should I involve the lighting designer in the process? 99
   Working with Costume Designers 100
   Costume and the Actor 101
   The Director and the Lighting Designer 101

6 Design – The Ear 103
  Music 103
  Sound 107

7 Casting the Play 109
  The Actor's World 109
  Do I Cast the Actor or the Part? 111
  The Audition Process 113
  Putting It Together 115

8 Awayday 2: Stanislavski and Actioning 117

9 To Cut or Not to Cut, That Is the Question 127
  Length 129
  Shape 130
  Choice of Edition 136

10 The Rehearsal Plan 139
  The Traditional Way of Organizing Rehearsals 140
  Basic Aims of Rehearsal 141
  Making a Plan 142
    Beginning 142
    Middle 144
    Nearly-at-the-end 146

11 Rehearsing the Play: Beginning 147
  The Rehearsal Room 147
  Stage Management 149
  An Approach to Day One of Rehearsals 151

12 Awayday 3: Improvisation 155
  Building a Company 156
  Building a Character 158

Developing Relationships and Exploring the World of the Play 161
Exploring Scenes and Situations in the Play without Using the Text 167

13 Rehearsing the Play: End of the Beginning 171
Work on Language 171
Work on Character 172

14 Rehearsing the Play: Middle 175
Aims for Middle Section of Rehearsals 176
Examples from Romeo and Juliet 176
'The Tank' 179
Blocking 183
Blocking Large-scale Scenes 188
Second Pass at Scenes 190
What to Do if Your Actors Get Inhibited or Stuck 193

15 Rehearsing the Play: End 197
First Run Through: How Does it Work? 198
How to Give Your Notes 200
Second and Third Run Throughs 202
Preparing for the Theatre 205

16 Tech, Dress, Previews and Opening 207
The 'Tech' 207
How to Set Up a Tech 208
The 'Dress' 212
Curtain Calls 215
Previews 216
Opening 219

Index 222

List of Figures

1 Axes: proscenium. Drawing courtesy of Adrian Noble 81
2 Doll's house. Drawing courtesy of Adrian Noble 91
3 Swan Theatre, Stratford-upon-Avon. Drawing courtesy of Adrian Noble 93
4 Tank. Drawing courtesy of Adrian Noble 180

Acknowledgements and Thanks

'What the fuck do you think you've got to offer in this business?'

These were the words that greeted me as I entered the old 'church' at the Drama Centre, London for my entrance interview. I don't remember my reply, but I remain eternally grateful to the three men sitting on the far side of the trestle table that day, the founder principals, Christopher Fettes, Yet Malmgren and John Blatchley, who are largely responsible for my dramatic education, my *formation*.

These were brave times. Theirs was a total, sometimes brutal, immersive education, which gave me, on the one hand, a methodology, and on the other, a real sense of myself as an artist. Vladimir Mirodan has recorded their work well in many books and articles, and Clive Barker, whose book *Theatre Games* is well worth a read, was an inspirational, anarchic inventor of games. Much of the work was Stanislavski-based and there are good versions of his key texts, *An Actor Prepares* and *Building a Character*, readily available.

I spent my summers in Paris until my money ran out and thank Jean-Louis Barrault and Madeleine Renaud for giving me my first experience of a professional rehearsal room. In term time, I spent my weekends at the BFI, the British Film Institute, and consumed voraciously the works of the great European masters, Buñuel, Bergman, Fellini, de Sica, Bertolucci, etc.

Richard Cottrell, Artistic Director of the Bristol Old Vic, was a great supporter and placed extraordinary trust in me as his Resident Director.

Michael Elliott invited me to the Manchester Royal Exchange to direct *The Duchess of Malfi*, a turning point in my career, and Peter Brook stepped in and enabled a French production in Paris. His book, *The Empty Space*, remains the most inspirational read for a young director.

Terry Hands and John Barton offered me a place at the Royal Shakespeare Company, in many ways, a homecoming. Read John's book *Playing Shakespeare*. Together with Trevor Nunn and Cicely Berry they opened windows onto the green pastures and peopled cities of Shakespeare's imagination and helped me identify those crucial connections between language and character. I would propose Cis's *The Actor and His Text* as a must read – thoughtful and bursting with practical applications.

For this book, I have used the excellent Arden Third Series for my references and thank Mark Dudgeon and the folk at The Arden Shakespeare for their welcome and sharp responses.

But most of all I must thank actors, many, many actors who have surprised, delighted, shocked and amazed me with their talent and generosity. Many are referred to in the pages of this book – Ralph Fiennes, Ken Branagh, Robert Stephens, Michael Gambon, Helen Mirren, David Suchet, Ben Kingsley; but I must add John Wood, Alan Rickman, Juliet Stevenson, Ray Fearon, Joanne Pearce, Derek Jacobi, Cheryl Campbell, Antony Sher, Penelope Wilton, Jonathan Pryce, Sinead Cusack, Simon Russell Beale and many more.

Finally, I thank the actors I worked with in North America, at Stratford Ontario and San Diego, whose boundless enthusiasm, raw talent and hunger for knowledge relit the fire of passion for Shakespeare that had, perhaps, faltered a little after several decades.

Introduction

A hidden soul seemed to be flowing forth from Rosamund's fingers; and so indeed it was, since souls live on in perpetual echoes, and to all fine expression there goes somewhere an originating activity, if it be only that of an interpreter.
–MIDDLEMARCH, GEORGE ELIOT

This book started life as a companion to *How to Do Shakespeare*, in which I attempted to provide a practical methodology for speaking and acting Shakespeare.

This book will attempt to provide a young director with the tools and practice that will allow him or her to successfully execute a production of a Shakespeare play.

It will take you through the narrative of directing a Shakespeare, step by step. It will give you a methodology that is applicable in most circumstances. We will start with the preparation of the text, cover the design process, casting and rehearsals, run throughs, lighting and sound, talk through the technical rehearsals and first encounters with an audience. En route, we will take three 'Awaydays' to focus on three subjects that are crucial to your success as a director: an analysis of Shakespeare's craft, 'how he does it', a practical study of improvisation and a basic appreciation of Stanislavski's Method.

You may be a student, or maybe just starting out in the profession, or an actor contemplating a switch to directing or anyone dreaming of a life in the theatre. Know this: by developing and sharpening your skills on a Shakespeare text, you will be preparing yourself for your next production, whatever or wherever that may be. This might be your very first production, as a student or in the professional theatre; it might take place in a studio or outside on a lawn; it might be a classic or a new play. It doesn't matter. Shakespeare was the source of most Western drama, and by learning how to direct his work, you are better positioning yourself for most challenges that will come your way as a director.

What follows will be largely practical, but partly philosophical, even political. Any production of any play is shaped by a vision of the world; the interplay of the writer's vision and the director's interpretation of it. Shakespeare had the ability to create whole worlds, complete cosmologies that frequently change and develop as the story progresses. I see the job of the director to help guide his/her colleagues through the story, into these different worlds and to allow access for our audience, emotionally, intellectually and, indeed, spiritually.

The director must therefore create an integrated whole that is logical to the text. You need to create a context on the stage in which the words and actions of the play *make sense*. This doesn't mean that it has to be done in period costume; that is another question. And it doesn't mean that you shouldn't cut or adapt the text. But it has to be rigorous and logical.

There's no doubt in my mind that Shakespeare is more difficult to direct than other playwrights, but the payback is immense. That is why the challenge of Shakespeare is the best possible preparation for a career in the theatre. It may be many years before you are entrusted with the resources to mount a Shakespeare production on the scale you might see at the Royal Shakespeare Company or the Lincoln Center. That has always been the case. But hone your skills and develop your own method of working as early as possible. This might be a student production with twenty actors or a fringe production with a cast of five. In many ways as a director, you should follow the path of maximum resistance! The greater the challenge, the greater the fear, the greater the reward.

For a young director, probably the greatest challenge will be working with the actor. It has certainly been my experience and, I suppose, my philosophy, that the key to success as a director is to understand the processes and priorities of the actor. To that end, you should seek to work with the very best actors possible. They may be in your class, or young actors starting out in the business or even at the top of their profession. They might well disagree with you sometimes, they might even be tricky to deal with, but if you respect their priorities and processes, they will respect you in turn and your work will benefit. Casting my first production at the RSC, Ostrovski's *The Forest*, I heard on the grapevine that Alan Howard was interested in playing the lead, the Tragedian. At that time, he was head and shoulders the company leading man. I was absolutely terrified of him. But I picked up the phone. Alan was charming, quite shy and totally dedicated to the work.

Ponder this for a moment:

If you saw Ian McKellan acting or heard him talking about acting, you would get a strong sense that he was part of a whole line of actors stretching back to Shakespeare's day and to Richard Burbage, who created many of his most famous roles. It can be assumed that the older, more experienced actors in the first productions of Shakespeare's plays passed on their skills to the younger members of the company. This relay race, this handing on of the baton from actor to actor, extended over the generations, developing and responding to different circumstances and audiences. I believe a core, practical knowledge of how to do Shakespeare is still there in the DNA of our present day acting community.

This, together with the relatively late arrival of the director on the theatrical scene, has meant that, in the UK, the actor has retained considerable power. Indeed, I remember a conversation with the Artistic Director of the RSC, when I was an assistant director. I asked him how I could get a show of my own to direct. 'Oh, get the actors to beat my door down for you to direct them.' That story is partly testament to the importance of 'company' in the RSC and partly a practical example of actor power. Most movies are only 'green lit' when actors agree to be in them.

A lot of this book will, therefore, focus on working with actors.

Acting Shakespeare is just as exciting and challenging as directing Shakespeare. You are their guide but, crucially, a fellow traveller. As a guide, a traveller, it's good to have a map or at least a sound understanding of the terrain. So we need to take a look at Shakespeare's world.

Shakespeare's vision of the world was largely drawn from a humanist tradition, with roots back into Medieval drama; a healing, integrated, classically based view of man's interaction with the world around him.

As directors, we live in a late capitalist world; society is fragmented, the individual feels alienated, tradition is mistrusted and is often used as a tool of oppression.

So how do we reconcile these? Do I take the work of Shakespeare and fragment it, reorder it, editorialize it so that it expresses my view of the world? Or should my point of departure be Shakespeare's world and my effort be to make his broad vision of humanity accessible, vivid and radical to a contemporary audience? Some would argue that the job of the director is to offer a critique of Shakespeare's work. I don't say that we should try to second guess a writer's intention but I do believe that the director must respect the writer, whether it be William Shakespeare or Samuel Beckett or Caryl Churchill. This comes down to why we do theatre and what is the role of the director.

As you approach your work, consider this: since the Second World War, a fundamental fault line has developed through most contemporary European theatre and, to a much lesser extent, North American theatre. I include here the world of opera in which alternative visions are, arguably, much more violently expressed onstage and attacked or appreciated from the auditorium. Opera production over the past forty to fifty years has been the canary in the coal mine. In opera, the director has taken a backseat on matters musical and the conductor has left the stage world to the director, sometimes very grudgingly! Given the imperative in postwar Germany for wholesale cultural reinvention, a strain of highly subsidized 'Regietheater', Director's Theatre, has emerged. This has been mostly supported by the Intendants of the opera houses and often loathed by the singers. Without question, some extraordinary work has been created. However, my experience of many of these productions is that they showcase the director's interpretation at the expense of the drama or the music. I would encourage and support bold, radical, contemporary interpretations, so long as they are rigorous and not merely opportunistic, masking sloppy thinking.

There is another tension or dialectic that you must consider.

Hamlet tells the actors newly arrived in Elsinore: 'We'll hear a play tomorrow.' Not 'see' but 'hear'. When did you last go and 'hear' a play? Of course, Elizabethan and Jacobean audiences enjoyed a good spectacle, but it seems self-evident that a fundamental shift in perception of drama has taken place over the past four hundred years.

Shakespeare's actors, we can presume, would start with the text, the words, rhythms, texture and meanings of the language and this would form the principal means of communication with the audience. Hence 'hear'. Any psychological or emotional interpretation or physical manifestation would emanate from the text. As the baton passed down over the centuries, an actor's skill set developed. Advances in science and technology have led to the explosion of cinema, a much more private experience than theatre. In parallel, the experiments and discoveries of Darwin and Freud allowed the work of Stanislavski, the great Russian actor, director and teacher. His analysis of the acting process and the methodology of training have revolutionized acting throughout most of the world. Stanislavski's Method is now the very oxygen that actors breathe, whether or not they subscribe to his teaching, or benefit from his training. We will take time to examine it in an Awayday. Put simply, Stanislavski's Method prescribes an 'inner' identification with a character, leading to a particular outward manifestation. This method is particularly well suited to film acting.

Compare this to Shakespeare's actors. *Outside in, or inside out.*

So a modern actor in receipt of the mythical baton inherits a wealth of seemingly contradictory knowledge. The director of a Shakespeare play must fully understand this tension because, as I will show, this offers him/her the most exciting and creative opportunities.

Finally ... I believe the director is first and foremost an artist, albeit an interpretive artist. Each production you embark upon has the potential to become a great work of art. It will be ephemeral but will stand in dynamic relationship to the source material – Shakespeare in this case. Take responsibility for your work, but keep moving forward. The great French actor/director Jean-Louis Barrault was generous and supportive to me in my student days; I remember his maxim: 'Feel passion for everything but cling to nothing.'

Where shall we start?

1

You

> *To thine own self be true*
> –HAMLET 1.3.77

Let's start with you. You are your own raw material. You can mine, develop, fashion and present your skills.

You must stand up and call yourself a director and pursue the roads that will lead you to production and success.

This requires courage and, perhaps, a degree of arrogance. You need energy, intellectual and emotional. Intellectually, it's hard work and can be frustrating, particularly if you are unsure of how to set about the job, i.e. if you have no methodology. This book will help you create your own methodology. Emotionally, it can be exhausting. But allow your emotions full rein, because emotion is the oil that allows the creative functions to operate, and emotion enables the connections to spark between idea and idea, image and image, concept and concept. So try to connect with the emotions that slosh around in your own life; they will help you to empathize with the emotions and predicaments of the characters in the play you are working on.

And, of course, you need luck.

I was lucky that the nascent National Theatre under Laurence Olivier was based, for a while, in Chichester where I grew up, giving me the opportunity to see the very great actors of the day: Olivier himself, Ralph Richardson, John Gielgud, Peggy Ashcroft, Robert Stephens and many more.

I was lucky that my first boss at the Bristol Old Vic, Richard Cottrell, was an extraordinarily generous and far-sighted producer, who gave me real responsibility and the opportunity to direct great classics in big spaces: *Titus Andronicus*, *The Changeling*, *Timon of Athens*, *A View from the Bridge* and more.

But it was not luck that led me to realize that university drama was a totally inadequate grounding for work in the professional theatre. Indeed it seemed to breed hubris and complacency. So I sought a proper training, Drama Centre, London, and set about finding the money to pay for it.

It was not luck that led me to the Royal Shakespeare Company. It was the obvious destination for a young director interested in the classics; but, crucially, I was content to join on the bottom rung, as an assistant director, and work my way up.

And it was not luck that led me to persuade Helen Mirren to play the Duchess of Malfi for me at the Manchester Royal Exchange. She was already a big, big star. It was terrifying, but a crucial, career-changing move that opened all sorts of doors and opportunities. I always tell my kids to look fear in the face!

Perhaps more important than anything, you need *instinct*.

The process of creativity, whether with a designer or in the rehearsal room with actors, requires great flexibility and the ability to improvise in the moment. I'm not talking about acting exercises; I'm talking about the ability to respond immediately and laterally to what's happening in the here and now; a new idea from the designer, a different interpretation of a speech from an actor. The dull director will plod on down his/her chosen path; the arrogant director will believe that every other contribution is of very limited importance compared to his/her own. This director will coerce, bully, perhaps charm his collaborators into accepting his interpretation.

Can you learn instinct? Do you either have it or do you not?

I believe you can work on your instinct. Here's a formula:

INSTINCT = IMAGINATION × EXPERIENCE

You can enrich your imagination and consciously set about widening your experience.

- Who or what inspires you? Study their work, feed off their work. Try to meet them.
- Glut yourself on film or theatre or dance or paintings.
- Try to cross frontiers. I mean quite literally: travel and experience the culture of other countries. We must be internationalist and open to challenge and influence from wheresoever.
- Also cross cultural frontiers. Consciously seek out experiences from genres that you, perhaps, do not feel comfortable with. Classical music perhaps? Performance art?

So I encourage you to enter different worlds, literally and imaginatively. Immerse yourself in different cultural experiences. Some might describe this as elitist. Ignore them. If you wish to develop as an artist, you must undertake journeys, particularly journeys of the imagination. You are not a social worker, you are an artist.

One of the greatest sources of experience is, of course, to practise. At school, at university or college, in amateur or semi-professional situations. Particularly seek out opportunities to act; try to get a real taste for it, the excitement, adrenalin buzz and satisfaction of performance. And try your hand at directing, wherever you can.

All this will add to your experience. But in the moment-by-moment communication and negotiation that is the rehearsal process, you will need craft and technique. A methodology.

Let's meet Shakespeare himself. Him.

2

Him

Let's think about him – your collaborator. Try to develop a dynamic relationship with him, as if he were living. Work together creatively. You can challenge him and he will challenge you.

Ask yourself why you are interested in directing his plays. The language is often tricky, sometimes quite obscure. The plots far-fetched, the predicaments of the characters are, sometimes, hard to relate to on first reading. On a practical level, his plays are hard to get on because they have larger than usual cast sizes and appear to require a high and particular level of skill from all concerned.

For some, they seem to emanate from a remote or alien culture.

Nevertheless, young artists and audiences around the world have found a mirror to their situation in his work, a conduit to or glimpse of a better world, or a process of moral enrichment or emotional healing. Shakespeare appears to cross international frontiers, racial differences, political divides, class distinctions. Artists and audiences have found resonance in London and New York, but also in Moscow and Poland under Soviet tyranny, Beijing, the prisons of apartheid South Africa and the favelas of Brazil.

So how is this the case and how does it affect you as a director?

Shakespeare was a frontiersman, an artistic explorer in the great age of global exploration and the beginnings of global exploitation. He was a real man of the Renaissance, when frontiers rolled back, scientific knowledge grew exponentially and European artists drew deep from the wells of Greek and Roman culture.

Crucially, for us, Shakespeare was a humanist. Think of the Globe Theatre, the original Globe of which he was a shareholder, sometime actor of small parts and principal playwright. Imagine yourself standing in the auditorium looking at an actor on the stage. From almost anywhere you stand or sit in that auditorium, you would have fellow human beings in your line of sight. An essentially democratic experience. Human beings side by side with other human beings.

This hasn't always been the case and certainly isn't nowadays. Think of the ancient Greek theatres at Epidauros or Taormina. An actor would have worn a mask and kathorni (a form of footwear that gives height and stature to the performer), both of which would have enlarged and amplified his presence. (The actors were all men.) Above him was the sky, in the distance, often, the sea, or hills or woods. Man in Nature.

After Shakespeare, when most performances moved inside, we get the Restoration and Georgian playhouses, in which the actor performed against artificial scenery, and the audience experience was calibrated according to their status or ability to pay. The richest get the best seats. Pretty undemocratic.

Think again of the Globe Theatre, the 'Wooden O'. Very little scenery, which perforce throws the emphasis onto the actor and particularly onto the text. Shakespeare told stories inside this 'O' and created whole worlds in the audience's imagination. These words are from the opening Chorus of *King Henry V*.

CHORUS
O for a Muse of fire, that would ascend
The brightest heaven of invention,
A kingdom for a stage, princes to act
And monarchs to behold the swelling scene!
Then should the warlike Harry, like himself,
Assume the port of Mars; and at his heels,
Leash'd in like hounds, should famine, sword and fire
Crouch for employment. But pardon, and gentles all,
The flat unraised spirits that have dared
On this unworthy scaffold to bring forth
So great an object: can this cockpit hold
The vasty fields of France? or may we cram
Within this wooden O the very casques
That did affright the air at Agincourt?
O, pardon! since a crooked figure may
Attest in little place a million;
And let us, ciphers to this great accompt,
On your imaginary forces work.

(*King Henry V* Prologue 1–18)

I love the use of the word 'work'. The text is active on the audience's imagination as yeast is active in the making of bread. Here the Chorus talks directly to the audience, looks them straight in the eye.

Shakespeare's subject is Humankind and with the Globe, they found the perfect space: on the one hand, practical and democratic because it housed thousands of people, from all walks of life, from all stations of society, all with a reasonable sight of the stage; on the other, an imaginative space which could conjure worlds though stories and poetry. And, best of all, the Globe was the perfect metaphor for the whole endeavour.

I very much hope that a part of you wants to become a director in order to change the world. Can drama change the world? Occasionally a play can so capture the imagination of the nation that it brings about political change. This usually takes place in the forum of TV drama. In the 1960s, Ken Loach's *Cathy Come Home* changed a nation's perception of the plight of the homeless. However, as I write this decades later, the stain of homelessness remains as vivid as ever. More often and perhaps more importantly, drama or a particular production can give voice to a political and cultural shift that is already underway. Ariane Mnouchkine's *1789*, produced in France in 1970, gave brilliant voice to the cultural/political revolution that had swept Paris in May 1968, the 'Evenements'. Tony Kushner's amazing diptych, *Angels in America* (1991) explored and helped to define a response to a catastrophic pandemic and thereby enabled individuals and communities to move on.

Where does Shakespeare fit into this? I will demonstrate in this book that his plays offer a paradigm of *change*. They show how a world can be transformed from one reality to another. In *As You Like It*, for example, an illegitimate, despotic regime is transformed into a more caring, loving society. The new world is marked by the celebration of marriages, offering the hope of new life. In the final Act of *Measure for Measure*, the Duke commands all parties to meet outside the city gates. In that great last act, all the confusions are resolved and all malefactors punished, allowing the possibility of healing. Only then are they fit to re-enter the city.

So Shakespeare offers the director models of change and offers an audience the opportunity to conceptualize change. If the story is well told, the journey an audience undergoes equips them with a heightened emotional intelligence.

Think of all this when you approach the text.

3

The Director and the Text

Part One: The World (Who's Who)

What is the world of the play?

This will govern everything that you do. The actors you seek to work with, the creative team you employ, the design you create, the way you rehearse, the music you use. Everything.

Let's start on page 1. Look at the **cast list**. Let's take a tragedy, a comedy and a history play. *Romeo and Juliet*, *A Midsummer Night's Dream* and *King Henry V*. Here's the cast list of *Romeo and Juliet*:

> ESCALUS, Prince of Verona.
> MERCUTIO, kinsman to the Prince, and friend to ROMEO.
> PARIS, a young Nobleman, kinsman to the Prince.
> Page to Paris.
> MONTAGUE, head of a Veronese family at feud with the Capulets.
> LADY MONTAGUE, wife to MONTAGUE.
> ROMEO, son to MONTAGUE.
> BENVOLIO, nephew to MONTAGUE, and friend to ROMEO.
> ABRAM, servant to MONTAGUE.

BALTHASAR, servant to ROMEO.
CAPULET, head of a Veronese family at feud with the Montagues.
LADY CAPULET, wife to CAPULET.
JULIET, daughter to CAPULET.
TYBALT, nephew to LADY CAPULET.
CAPULET'S COUSIN, an old man.
NURSE to JULIET.
PETER, servant to Juliet's Nurse.
SAMPSON, servant to CAPULET.
GREGORY, servant to CAPULET.
Servants.
FRIAR LAWRENCE, a Franciscan.
FRIAR JOHN, of the same Order.
An Apothecary.
CHORUS.
Three Musicians.
An Officer.
Citizens of Verona; several Men and Women, relations to both houses; Maskers, Guards, Watchmen and Attendants.

I always encourage my students, in a workshop situation, to state the obvious. State the obvious and **write it down**! The directing process usually lasts several months and it's very easy to lose sight of the wood for the trees. It's useful to have something to remind yourself of your early thoughts if and when you get stuck!

So, what's obvious?

They seem to have **Italianate** names.

There are three **families**-not two but three – the Montagues, the Capulets and the aristocratic family of Prince Escalus. He mentions wives, daughters, sons, nephews, kinsmen.

Look for social **hierarchy**. There's a Prince, his kinsmen Mercutio and Paris and two other families, presumably lower down the social scale ('Both alike in dignity' we soon learn); there are several servants, all connected to these families; and a couple of Catholic priests.

Gender; there are a lot more men than women. You will certainly have to take a line on this issue. It's really important and we'll deal with it.

So here you have a world, totally recognizable to Shakespeare's audience and to most audiences in the twenty-first century.

With that cast list, ask yourself what is the **subject** of the play likely to be? I'd guess **domestic politics**, **relationships**, **particularly relationships inside the family**. He uses the word 'feud', so we are talking explosive, violent, possibly loving. Make a list of the subjects that strike you. *Write it down*. It's your job to create a world in which these relationships are *logical*.

Let's move on. Here's *A Midsummer Night's Dream*:

> THESEUS, Duke of Athens
> HIPPOLYTA, Queen of the Amazons, bethrothed to THESEUS
> EGEUS, Father to HERMIA
> HERMIA, daughter to EGEUS, in love with LYSANDER
> HELENA, in love with DEMETRIUS
> LYSANDER, in love with HERMIA
> DEMETRIUS, in love with HERMIA
> PHILOSTRATE, Master of the Revels to THESEUS
>
> QUINCE, the Carpenter
> SNUG, the Joiner
> BOTTOM, the Weaver
> FLUTE, the Bellows-mender

SNOUT, the Tinker
STARVELING, the Tailor
OBERON, King of the Fairies
TITANIA, Queen of the Fairies
PUCK, or robin goodfellow, a Fairy
PEASEBLOSSOM, Fairy
COBWEB, Fairy
MOTH, Fairy
MUSTARDSEED, Fairy
PYRAMUS, THISBE, WALL, MOONSHINE, LION; Characters in the Interlude performed by the Clowns

Other Fairies attending their King and Queen
Attendants on Theseus and Hippolyta

State the obvious.

Some of the names are **Greek**, possibly **Ancient Greek** and some **English**.

Here's a play with **mortal** beings – Dukes, carpenters, children, etc. – and **immortal** beings, fairies.

Shakespeare also seems to be using names as part **character descriptions**: Snug, Snout, etc. These people seem to have real jobs as tradesmen and craftsmen. Some of the fairy names, like Cobweb or Moth, might refer to their physical characteristics.

As in *Romeo and Juliet*, there are **families**, or rather one father and a daughter. Perhaps not so significant.

But there are **husbands and wives**, or **lovers**. There seem to be at least four couples.

There appears to be a **hierarchy** amongst the mortals and the immortals: Dukes, lovers and working people and fairy aristocracy and ordinary fairies.

The mortal world and the immortal world have clear **parallels**. They seem to mirror each other. So for my production of the *Dream*, I decided that the cast of mortals would double as Fairies and that I would use the same space for court and forest/fairyland.

There are clearly overlaps with *Romeo and Juliet*, some subjects that strongly interest him. Fathers and daughters, lovers, the social order, a somewhat exotic setting. (Remember, it would be highly unlikely for members of Shakespeare's audience to travel to Italy or Greece.)

So what might the **subject** be?

I think the clue lies in the young lovers. Two of the boys are in love with the same girl, Hermia. There's obviously confusion and tension here. He's talking about **love**, **betrothal** and, we discover, the bumpy road to **marriage**.

And, unlike the world of *R and J*, here he conjures a visible and an invisible world. He has gone beyond what we might call 'realism'. There's also a clue in the reference to an 'Interlude'; a short play within the play. Your imagination can start connecting all these dots!

Finally, here's *King Henry V*:

> KING HENRY V.
> DUKE OF CLARENCE, brother to the King.
> DUKE OF BEDFORD, brother to the King.
> DUKE OF GLOUCESTER, brother to the King.
> DUKE OF EXETER, uncle to the King.
> DUKE OF YORK, cousin to the King.

EARL OF SALISBURY.

EARL OF HUNTINGDON.

EARL OF WESTMORELAND.

EARL OF WARWICK.

ARCHBISHOP OF CANTERBURY.

BISHOP OF ELY.

EARL OF CAMBRIDGE.

LORD SCROOP.

SIR THOMAS GREY.

SIR THOMAS ERPINGHAM, officer in KING HENRY'S army.

GOWER, officer in KING HENRY'S army.

FLUELLEN, officer in KING HENRY'S army.

MACMORRIS, officer in KING HENRY'S army.

JAMY, officer in KING HENRY'S army.

BATES, soldier in the same.

COURT, soldier in the same.

WILLIAMS, soldier in the same.

PISTOL.

NYM.

BARDOLPH.

BOY.

a herald.

CHARLES VI, king of France.

LEWIS, the Dauphin.

DUKE OF BERRY.

DUKE OF BRITTANY.

DUKE OF BURGUNDY.

DUKE OF ORLEANS.

DUKE OF BOURBON.

The Constable of France.

RAMBURES, French Lord.

GRANDPRÉ, French Lord.

Governor of Harfleur

MONTJOY, a French herald.

Ambassadors to the King of England.

ISABEL, queen of France.

KATHARINE, daughter to Charles and Isabel.

ALICE, a lady attending on her.

HOSTESS of a tavern in Eastcheap, formerly Mistress Nell Quickly, and now married to Pistol.

CHORUS.

Lords, Ladies, Officers, Soldiers, Citizens, Messengers, and Attendants.

By any standards, this is a huge cast. It's evidently a play of epic proportions. So let's try and break it down into its constituent ingredients. State the obvious!

The cast list divides into two significant groups, the **English** and the **French**.

Both groups contain large numbers of **aristocrats**.

The **social span** on the English side, however, is much wider. Apart from the King, there are Dukes, Knights, Bishops, officers and common soldiers.

Break this down further and we find that, amongst the officers there is an Englishman, a Welshman, an Irishman and a Scotsman, Gower, Fluellen, MacMorris and Jamy. We find three ordinary soldiers and a small group with exotic sounding names, Pistol, Nym and Bardolph.

There are no commoners in the French list.

There's only one Englishwoman, a commoner, and three French, all aristocrats.

There is a character called **Chorus**.

This all reveals a huge amount about the **subject** of the play, before you've read a single word.

Clearly, on one level, the subject is going to be **war** or **conflict**. But the detail of the cast list suggests something different or certainly more nuanced. Shakespeare seems to be setting up an exploration of a whole society, certainly on the English side. So perhaps the subject matter is more about **cultural identity**, particularly when he introduces such specific national identities amongst the soldiers.

The presence of a Chorus gives us a strong hint as to the **stylistic framework** he had in mind.

It's worth noting that in all three of these cast lists, there is a powerful conflict built in. *Romeo* and *Juliet*, *Montagues* and *Capulets*, *Mortals* and *Immortals*, *French* and *English*. This idea of **juxtaposition** or **apposition** is central to the whole of Shakespeare's thinking. In his verse and in his dramaturgy, he loved to place word next to word, phrase next to phrase, idea next to idea, scene next to contrasting scene. This all creates dramatic energy.

Part Two: Reading the Play

Ok, now let's read the play.

I find it very hard to read a Shakespeare play in a single sitting, but read it over as short a period of time as possible.

There will be masses you don't fully understand at first; don't worry. You will find that directing a Shakespeare play is an iterative process.

Every time you return to the text, you will understand more and your vision of the play will change and develop.

First of all, **concentrate on the story**.

Write down the story in as concise a way as possible. Don't try and include every detail, just the broad brush strokes. See if you can **tell the story in just three sentences**. Three movements if you like, **beginning, middle and end**.

Try this exercise on the three plays we have chosen.

Romeo and Juliet:

1. Romeo meets Juliet, the daughter of his sworn enemy, and falls in love.
2. They marry in secret, violence erupts between the two families, forcing the newlywed Romeo into exile.
3. The 'cunning plan' devised by Friar Lawrence, their priest, to resolve all the problems, goes disastrously wrong, leading to the suicide of the lovers.

Of course, this is an over-simplification, but it forces you to **concentrate on the main action**.

Let's try it with *Henry V*.

1. Henry declares war on France.
2. The war rages in France, leading to a famous victory at Agincourt.
3. A peace treaty is signed, sealed by a marriage between the English King and the French Princess.

(It's worth noting that each part, beginning, middle and end, is not of the same length. 'Middle' is considerably longer than the other two.)

And *A Midsummer Night's Dream*:

1. The lovers flee Athens in search of true love.
2. Chaos and confusion reigns in the woods.
3. A triple wedding is celebrated.

This is a tricky one, because there are parallel stories, parallel realities. It is useful, however, to **identify the strongest narrative thrust of the drama, because it is *that* the audience will latch onto and follow.** You will discover that audiences are like truffle hounds; they will hunt down the main story, whatever obstacle you may throw in their way. If your production is not paying attention to the main story, you will start to lose their attention.

I use this exercise, beginning, middle and end, constantly for two reasons. Firstly, it *forces* me to concentrate my ideas on the forward dramatic thrust. Secondly, it helps me to identify the structure of a play, and this points to the meaning of the play.

And don't be shy of using **labels** or **titles** for sections. For the *Dream* it might be Flight, Confusion and Weddings. At the Royal Shakespeare Company we used to give names to scenes or whole sections. The stage management, in particular, found this very helpful. It provided quick, clear communication for the actors and the whole backstage staff. 'Company, stage staff, props, LX, sound, stand by for Triple Wedding. Stand by please.' The whole building would hear this over the tannoy system. Everyone knew exactly what was happening!

Part Three: Analysing the Play

Let's pick up on this idea of labelling scenes or sections. You may notice that a pattern has emerged in our simple **three-step analysis**.

Like **apposition**, this is a tool that Shakespeare used constantly throughout his working life.

The story of the above three plays could be described in three words:

Crisis
Confusion
Resolution

This is a paradigm that applies to most of his work – *King Lear*, *Tempest*, *Twelfth Night*, etc.

How does it work?

Each play starts off with a **crisis**.

Hermia is told by her father that, if she does not marry the boy of *his* choice, she faces death or a life in a convent. She decides to elope. It's **a life or death situation**, even though the genre is comedic and the subject is love.

In *Henry V*, the crisis is the **declaration of war**.

The love between Romeo and Juliet, the scions of two feuding families, propels the action into crisis. This is no ordinary love, this is **life changing, world changing**.

In the forest in *A Midsummer Night's Dream*, there is **confusion**. Lover loses lover, weird and wonderful things are engineered by the fairy, Puck. It's night time, violent, chaotic and very scary.

In *Henry V*, the bloody campaign unfolds in violence, confusion and fear.

The feud in *RJ* boils over onto the streets. Violence, exile, sexually charged, passionate love.

With the dawn in the *Dream*, all is **resolved**. Three marriages are celebrated. **Resolution and harmony**.

After the reading of the names of the dead and the singing of the Te Deum, Henry V marries the Princess of France. **Resolution and Peace**. In my production of *H5* with Ken Branagh, I marked the end of the second movement, the end of the war, with a mighty version of the Te Deum composed by Howard Blake, and the image of Henry lifting the dead body of the boy and carrying him out diagonally across the battlefield.

The resolution of *R and J* is **tragic and inevitable**, a double suicide.

Not only is each crisis a matter of life and death, either literally or metaphorically, but none of them is anticipated. They come out of the blue, they ambush the audience. You can help to dramatize this, and provide a spur into the action. How? Apply the **First Time** rule. It's the first time that Romeo and Juliet have felt like this, it's the first time the 'death or convent' law has been used in the *Dream*, etc.

The **confusions** are interesting. Shakespeare transports his characters into a different landscape: the battlefields of France, the forest outside Athens, the violent streets (and bedrooms) of Verona. In each case, Shakespeare adjusts and shifts the reality.

We know from documentaries of the First World War that a battlefield quickly becomes a quagmire, that the troops faced their future with a mixture of comradeship and terror. Shakespeare additionally places much of the action at night and so creates an authentic nightmare. (It's worth noting that Shakespeare had an uncanny insight into the conditions and psychology of the common soldier. Where he learnt this, we can only speculate.)

In the *Dream*, he chooses a forest at night time. It's dark, confusing and terrifying!

The street violence in *R and J* leads to banishment, the nightmare scenario of a bigamous marriage, fake poison, real poison. Again much action takes place at night.

R and J **resolves** in death, the *Dream* in marriage and therefore the possibility of children and *Henry V* with marriage and the hope of peace.

Let's focus on Shakespeare's use of the **forest**.

It's quite literal with the *Dream* and, say, *As You Like It*, but think of it as a **metaphor** as well. The battlefields of France are a forest, the heath in *King Lear* is a forest, the underworld, the 'stews' in Vienna in *Measure for Measure* is a forest. As Orlando points out in *As You Like It*, 'There's no clock in the forest' and it's very easy to get lost. You'll find it hard to walk in a straight line. The forest or wilderness offers the playwright and the director comic opportunities in the *Dream*, or a means of confronting the characters with experiences at the very edge of human suffering, as in *Lear* or *Macbeth*.

Disorientation in a forest affects a character's values as well; **their emotional equilibrium is disturbed**. What was certain becomes uncertain. **The forest is literal and psychological at the same time**. Hamlet does not enter a forest, but he embarks on a journey that takes him into dark and dangerous places from which he emerges to face his destiny: 'The readiness is all.'

This is very exciting territory for the director and extends into all areas of his/her work. Obviously with the **designer**; this analysis helps you to free yourself from the 'literal', so, in *Hamlet*, instead of just thinking of Elsinore as a series of rooms that contain the action, perhaps you might consider a landscape that changes and develops with Hamlet's psychological progress. (We'll extend this thinking much further in Chapter 6 on design.)

You will also find it of enormous help when working with the **actors** in the rehearsal room. Shakespeare's characters are frequently required to undertake the most extraordinary **journeys**; some quite literal, like Pericles, and some psychological. This is highly challenging stuff and you must be their companion and often their guide. You need to be sensitive to the emotional vulnerability that this journey can engender. There will also be times when you will need to encourage or even push an actor into uncomfortable territory.

You will find that actors very often think of their parts in terms of the **journey** of their character and may well accept or refuse a role accordingly. The longer the journey for the character, the better. If the Mechanicals in the *Dream* have regularly performed in front of a posh audience, or, indeed, regularly performed plays, then there is little at stake. If we witness the *very first time* they have performed, then their scenes can bristle with excitement. We will see each character grow and blossom. The parts become highly rewarding.

And for the audience, I believe this journey through Crisis, Confusion and Resolution is a source of great satisfaction. They probably won't be conscious of it, but the crisis will grab their attention, a matter of life or death; you will pitch them into confusion, the forest, a dangerous place, full of unexpected twists and turns on the path; finally you arrive at a resolution, which will be cathartic and enriching.

So it's important for everyone that you conceive this journey clearly and boldly prior to rehearsals, and keep referring back to it as you progress from day to day. Keep your eye on the wood, not just the trees!

(In **film**, which is usually shot out of order, it is vital for the director to keep in mind the bigger picture. Where does this 20-second shot fit into the overall cut? What should be the rhythm or emotional intensity? Here again, the director needs to be on top of the journey of the film.)

Part Four: Entering Shakespeare's World

Let us return to the first question of this section: what is the world of the play?

It's important to understand, as fully as possible, the world of the play as Shakespeare *imagined* it, even if, at a later stage, you choose to take your production in a completely different direction. That is your prerogative as a director. But, please, don't proceed in ignorance!

So what do we mean by **the world of the play?**

I mean the **social relationships, the political system and the religious framework** that underpin the action of a particular play. You need to consider the **intellectual frontiers** (e.g. did they believe the world was round or flat?), the **class relationships** (quite different in Elizabethan to twenty-first-century London) and the **spiritual beliefs** of the characters (e.g. do they believe in Heaven and Hell?).

You will need to assess the implication of all this on the **crucial constructs** of the society; **what are its values**, what are the **hopes**, what creates **fear**?

Furthermore, it will help you to get a handle on the **style** or **genre** that Shakespeare has chosen, or developed, for each play. Put simply, this is the relationship between the story and the audience. Is it comic, tragic, romantic, or something else?

You will need to consider how the characters think, how they express themselves, how their emotions work, their spiritual lives. Don't assume that everyone is just like you! One of the great joys of directing lies in the opportunities to enter different worlds and engage with people quite different from yourself.

All of the above can be deduced from the text and some simple supplementary research.

Once more, let's start with the **cast list**. Consider the characters **not just as individuals but as groups**.

I often start with **family trees**. Who is related to whom? Mothers, fathers, siblings, cousins, nephews, nieces. On a big piece of paper or cardboard, draw a diagram of everyone in the play and how they relate. This is fascinating and terribly revealing. In *R and J* there are three extended family groups. In the *Dream* there are few family groups. Leave some blank spaces on your chart. Do any of the Mechanicals have wives or families at home? Where is Hermia's mother? In *Henry V* you will need to work carefully to ascertain exactly who is related to whom amongst the aristocracy. There are real surprises here as, not unlike the present Royal Family, there are all sorts of connections by marriage and by birth which reveal kinships, betrayals, friendships, etc. Research into the family tree gave us powerful motivation when staging Act 2 Scene 2, the discovery and punishment of the traitors Cambridge, Grey and Scroop. Henry would have known them since childhood. He is incensed by the treachery of school friends who have abused their position and privilege. So, instead of cutting the scene as is often the case, we played it in full and gleaned great rewards.

All this is of immediate, practical use to actors and it will affect the way characters relate in the rehearsal room and ultimately onstage. It will help you set an agenda and work out some exercises prior to rehearsal.

As you reflect upon these family groups, start to consider how their behaviour *differs* from and how it is *similar* to modern families. It's hard to imagine a contemporary Western father threatening his daughter with death as in the *Dream*. But is this possible in other parts of the world? The family rows in *R and J* seem all too modern, but, even here, the authority of the father is altogether more potent than in many modern Western societies. Or is it? Dig deeper. Shakespeare has created a *patriarchal society* and in one way or another, this needs to be reflected in your production.

It will certainly help you to research family relationships in sixteenth- and seventeenth-century England and particularly their attitudes towards marriage, preferably a love bond, but, more importantly, a financial and social alliance. This will help you to understand the **logic** of Romeo and Juliet's actions, or Petruchio's in *Taming of the Shrew*.

Again, I stress, I am not advocating productions set strictly in the period in which he was writing (although this can be fascinating and elicit very strong responses from the audience). I am saying: **understand the world of the play, the logic of the action and make your production equally logical.**

Now move on to other groups: **friendship groups, work groups, class groupings**. I also find it useful to visualize this on paper. Who's friends with whom? What kind of friendship? How does this cross over with family groups? There are strong friendship groups in *R and J* and in the *Dream*. These are frequently **passionate friendships** that define the relationship. Mercutio is willing to die for his friend Romeo. This action helps define the world. There is a highly colourful group of friends towards the end of the *Henry V* cast list: the low life! Pistol, Nym, Bardolph and Mistress Quickly – drinking pals of Sir John Falstaff, denizens of London's East End. Here a bit of research into the *Henry IV* plays will help to define the world they inhabit and their relationship with Henry V himself.

It's vital to appreciate the **class groupings** in his plays. The English aristocracy functioned on a strict hierarchy, as, in many ways, it still does. Look at the cast list of *Henry V*: the king is first, the common people last. The **status** of each character influences every aspect of their personality, their actions and interactions with others: how they speak, whom they speak to, how they address them, their body language, their assumptions about their position in the world and their hopes and fears.

I have found it very useful to explore status thoroughly in rehearsal and your actors will welcome specific background information and research, in addition to status exercises which can also be very helpful.

Gender groupings are an area you will need to think about very carefully. For obvious reasons, Shakespeare wrote fewer female parts than male. However, there are wonderful examples of deep, passionate friendships, like Rosalind and Celia in *As You Like It*, as well as romantic or sibling rivalries. The relationships between the women in the plays are invariably brilliantly and unsentimentally drawn and are hugely rewarding to artist and audience alike. You will certainly want to increase the number of roles available to women as much as possible. We'll address this later in the book.

Much of your exploration of character *must* be conducted collaboratively with your actors. We'll discuss in detail the creation of biographies and the development of characterization in later chapters.

Let us pose, once again, the central question: **what kind of world do these characters inhabit**? What kind of story do they tell? From our analysis of cast and structure, the 'journey' of the play, we have sufficient information to answer this. Let's try.

Romeo and Juliet is a domestic **tragedy**, full of detailed relationships, social background, violent family intrigue, passionate sexual and romantic encounters, set in a patriarchal society in Italy. It is an urban play. It ends in death. I set my production in a small town in Sicily before the First World War. A traditional concept but one that resonates perfectly.

A Midsummer Night's Dream is a **comedy** of vivid contrasts, of magic and fantasy, of love and hope, of the pain of youth, where the everyday actions of this world jostle and rub up against an 'invisible' world. This is largely a rural play and it end in marriage and harmony. I created a world that appeared modern but eschewed contemporary social realism.

Henry V tells the **epic story** of the birth of a nation. We are in the realm of politics, conflict and the realities of war and soldiering. The play takes place in an international arena. It ends with the prospect of peace. I chose to set my production in the time of the real Henry V.

I have given each a different label. A **tragedy** tells a story that conducts an audience to the very frontier of human suffering and to the inevitable consequence, death. From the time of the ancient Greeks, this form has enabled society to confront their own mortality. A **comedy** tells a story about the very life forces that beat at the heart of our existence. The search for happiness and the desire for immortality through children. An **epic story**, whether it's *Henry V*, the *Aeneid*, *Paradise Lost* or *Game of Thrones*, will tell the story of a people or nation and the forces that shape their destiny.

Each of the worlds in our three texts is **real**. It's not that one is more or less artificial than the other. They are quite different and they each have a particular form of **energy** which you and your actors need to recognize and embrace. Each play offers a '360-degree' universe, with rulers and common people. But the **'feel'** of each play is quite different.

Before rehearsals begin, it's important to further define the 'feel' of the world and to identify **in concrete terms** how Shakespeare has achieved this.

You will find that each story is driven by actions of an **extreme** nature. In the *Dream*, the lovers elope in the middle of the night, Henry declares war over a tennis ball insult and the love of Romeo and Juliet is all-consuming and they must marry *immediately*. The fuel that drives these actions is pretty high octane, whether the paradigm, the journey, leads us to marriage or to death or to international conquest.

Consider these words of Rosalind in *As You Like It*, where she is addressing Orlando with whom she's fallen passionately in love. Remember, Rosalind is dressed as a *boy* at this point.

> ROSALIND
>
> Love is merely a madness, and, I tell you, deserves
> as well a dark house and a whip as madmen do: and
> the reason why they are not so punished and cured
> is, that the lunacy is so ordinary that the whippers
> are in love too.
>
> (*As You Like It* 3.2.288–392)

And these, where Rosalind is talking privately to her best friend, Celia, about how much she loves Orlando.

> ROSALIND
>
> O coz, coz, coz, my pretty little coz, that thou
> didst know how many fathom deep I am in love! But
> it cannot be sounded: my affection hath an unknown
> bottom, like the bay of Portugal.

CELIA

> Or rather, bottomless, that as fast as you pour
> affection in, it runs out.

ROSALIND

> No, that same wicked bastard of Venus that was begot
> of thought, conceived of spleen and born of madness,
> that blind rascally boy that abuses every one's eyes
> because his own are out, let him be judge how deep I
> am in love. I'll tell thee, Aliena, I cannot be out
> of the sight of Orlando: I'll go find a shadow and
> sigh till he come.

CELIA

> And I'll sleep.
>
> (As You Like It 4.1.195–208)

Rosalind describes love as an extreme, dangerous, all-consuming emotion. Love is a madness, love inhabits the Bay of Portugal, now called the Bay of Biscay, the most dangerous ocean for the Elizabethan sailor, a sea in which you are drawn under the surface and drown.

Dark, dangerous emotions, over which you have no control. You are blind and sick with love. Shakespeare uses this to comic effect in the *Dream* and tragic in *R and J*.

So look for *extreme actions and decisions*. This will help you create the appropriate world and set the **'oven'** of your production at the **right temperature**.

Now let's examine the **imaginative** world of the play. By this I don't just mean the presence of ghosts and fairies. The extraordinary feature of the Shakespearean theatre is its ability to transport you into the inner lives of the characters. So we understand them by their actions but also by their thoughts.

Look at this speech by Juliet. This is her wedding night. She has secretly married Romeo and is awaiting him in her bedroom.

JULIET

> Gallop apace, you fiery-footed steeds,
> Towards Phoebus' lodging: such a wagoner
> As Phaethon would whip you to the west,
> And bring in cloudy night immediately.
> Spread thy close curtain, love-performing night,
> That runaway's eyes may wink and Romeo
> Leap to these arms, untalk'd of and unseen.
> Lovers can see to do their amorous rites
> By their own beauties; or, if love be blind,
> It best agrees with night. Come, civil night,
> Thou sober-suited matron, all in black,
> And learn me how to lose a winning match,
> Play'd for a pair of stainless maidenhoods:
> Hood my unmann'd blood, bating in my cheeks,
> With thy black mantle; till strange love, grown bold,
> Think true love acted simple modesty.
> Come, night; come, Romeo; come, thou day in night;
> For thou wilt lie upon the wings of night
> Whiter than new snow on a raven's back.
> Come, gentle night, come, loving, black-brow'd night,
> Give me my Romeo; and, when he shall die,
> Take him and cut him out in little stars,
> And he will make the face of heaven so fine
> That all the world will be in love with night
> And pay no worship to the garish sun.
> O, I have bought the mansion of a love,
> But not possess'd it, and, though I am sold,

> Not yet enjoy'd: so tedious is this day
> As is the night before some festival
> To an impatient child that hath new robes
> And may not wear them.
>
> (*Romeo and Juliet* 3.2.1–31)

This speech is a highway into her imagination and is crucial to the creation of the world of the play. The interesting thing from our perspective is not that she is passionate, frustrated and wilful but that the **imagery** she uses reeks of death and sexual awakening. She wants to embrace darkness and night as a lover. The imagery leads the audience into these dark, dangerous realms. This is, of course, one of the great characteristics and opportunities of poetic drama: poetry can create worlds within worlds, realities within realities that echo and clash in our imagination. So the **language** of the play helps create the **world** of the play.

Look at another example. Here's Titania clashing with her husband, Oberon at their first meeting in *A Midsummer Night's Dream*.

> TITANIA
> These are the forgeries of jealousy:
> And never, since the middle summer's spring,
> Met we on hill, in dale, forest or mead,
> By paved fountain or by rushy brook,
> Or in the beached margent of the sea,
> To dance our ringlets to the whistling wind,
> But with thy brawls thou hast disturb'd our sport.
> Therefore the winds, piping to us in vain,
> As in revenge, have suck'd up from the sea
> Contagious fogs; which falling in the land
> Have every pelting river made so proud

That they have overborne their continents:
The ox hath therefore stretch'd his yoke in vain,
The ploughman lost his sweat, and the green corn
Hath rotted ere his youth attain'd a beard;
The fold stands empty in the drowned field,
And crows are fatted with the murrion flock;
The nine men's morris is fill'd up with mud,
And the quaint mazes in the wanton green
For lack of tread are undistinguishable:
The human mortals want their winter here;
No night is now with hymn or carol blest:
Therefore the moon, the governess of floods,
Pale in her anger, washes all the air,
That rheumatic diseases do abound:
And thorough this distemperature we see
The seasons alter: hoary-headed frosts
Far in the fresh lap of the crimson rose,
And on old Hiems' thin and icy crown
An odorous chaplet of sweet summer buds
Is, as in mockery, set: the spring, the summer,
The childing autumn, angry winter, change
Their wonted liveries, and the mazed world,
By their increase, now knows not which is which:
And this same progeny of evils comes
From our debate, from our dissension;
We are their parents and original.

(*A Midsummer Night's Dream* 2.1.81–117)

Here, again, a world is created by the poetry. The imagery is concrete, by which I mean specific, particular and, in this case, conjures up the whole natural world. The audience are led to **visualize** the world and the devastation caused by the quarrel between fairy King and Queen. Titania is **empowered** by this speech and thereafter we perceive her as a conjuror and the source of magic in the play, quite equal to Oberon. Which, of course, is why it's vital that the actor playing the role has the talent and know-how to communicate this fully! And you, the director, can certainly help.

Let's stay with the idea that **language** can help you define the world.

Let's look for some further examples at the other end of the social scale. Here are two examples from *Henry V*. Firstly an encounter between Pistol and his old drinking buddies, Nym and Bardolph. Mistress Quickly has jilted Nym and married Pistol, hence the bad feeling.

BARDOLPH
> Here comes Ancient Pistol and his wife: good
> corporal, be patient here. How now, mine host Pistol!

PISTOL
> Base tike, call'st thou me host? Now, by this hand,
> I swear, I scorn the term; Nor shall my Nell keep lodgers.

HOSTESS
> No, by my troth, not long; for we cannot lodge and
> board a dozen or fourteen gentlewomen that live
> honestly by the prick of their needles, but it will
> be thought we keep a bawdy house straight.
>
> **NYM and PISTOL draw**
> O well a day, Lady, if he be not drawn now! we
> shall see wilful adultery and murder committed.

BARDOLPH
> Good lieutenant! good corporal! offer nothing here.

NYM

Pish!

PISTOL

Pish for thee, Iceland dog! thou prick-ear'd cur of Iceland!

HOSTESS

Good Corporal Nym, show thy valour, and put up your sword.

NYM

Will you shog off? I would have you solus.

PISTOL

'Solus,' egregious dog? O viper vile!
The 'solus' in thy most mervailous face;
The 'solus' in thy teeth, and in thy throat,
And in thy hateful lungs, yea, in thy maw, perdy,
And, which is worse, within thy nasty mouth!
I do retort the 'solus' in thy bowels;
For I can take, and Pistol's cock is up,
And flashing fire will follow.

(*King Henry V* 2.1.25–51)

This exchange is, of course, in **prose**, and so has the rhythm and cadence of everyday speech. But the vocabulary and the phrasing is, to our ear, exotic and pungent and conjures up the dense underworld of Elizabethan London. It's a rare, spicy patois and for us, its significance lies as much in the **sound** as the **meaning**. The meaning is, in fact, very interesting and may require a bit of translating! And the choice of vocabulary and imagery tells us a lot about the peacockery and pretension of the characters and the alpha male world they inhabit. Shakespeare laughs at them but cares for them at the same time.

Compare this with a speech by Williams, a common soldier, in the middle of the night, on the eve of the battle of Agincourt. The English are outnumbered four to one. The **King**, visiting the troops in disguise claims:

> methinks I could not die any where so
> contented as in the king's company; his cause being
> just and his quarrel honourable.

Williams answers:

> WILLIAMS
> But if the cause be not good, the king himself hath
> a heavy reckoning to make, when all those legs and
> arms and heads, chopped off in battle, shall join
> together at the latter day and cry all 'We died at
> such a place;' some swearing, some crying for a
> surgeon, some upon their wives left poor behind
> them, some upon the debts they owe, some upon their
> children rawly left. I am afeard there are few die
> well that die in a battle; for how can they
> charitably dispose of any thing, when blood is their
> argument? Now, if these men do not die well, it
> will be a black matter for the king that led them to
> it; whom to disobey were against all proportion of
> subjection.
>
> <div align="right">(<i>King Henry V</i> 4.1.132–145)</div>

This is direct, articulate and to the point. The character of Williams is in precise focus, as are his arguments. We understand the man and we understand the situation. The world of this encounter is as '*real*' as any twentieth-century war movie. We don't worry as to whether a common soldier could argue with this articulacy. We have here an almost documentary style of theatre.

To conclude, **Shakespeare's characters are defined by what they say and how they say it, as much as by what they do and how they do it**. To which end, let's focus on the nuts and bolts of his writing. Let's understand **how he does it**.

Let's take our first Awayday.

4

Awayday 1: Dramatic Energy (How Does He Do It?)

What is emerging already is that Shakespeare was a supreme **craftsman**, and an appreciation of his skill and technique will help enormously in the preparation of your production.

Let's dig a bit deeper.

In any passage of Shakespearean text, there are seven basic elements you should learn to look out for. These are:

1. Apposition (the juxtaposition of words, phrases and ideas)
2. Metaphor (similes, metaphors, classical allusions and flights of fancy)
3. Metre and pulse
4. Line endings
5. Word play (rhyme, alliteration and assonance)

6   Vocabulary

7   Shape and structure.

I examine these in great detail in my book *How to do Shakespeare*, but I'll give you an essential guide here. I describe these seven elements as the **plumbing**:

> Plumbing is a useful analogy because pipes carry an essential commodity, water, all around the house and, by and large, are invisible. These seven elements are also essential because they carry the meaning, the character, the atmosphere and the cosmology of the play. It's a hugely valuable lesson to learn the basics of the plumbing, to learn the rules and the do's and don'ts of the craft, because they will give you the power and authority to appreciate the magnificence of the building, the play.

Let's examine the seven elements of Shakespeare's language.

Apposition

Consider for a moment the most famous words in the English language, possibly in all world literature:

HAMLET
    To be, or not to be, that is the question:
    Whether 'tis nobler in the mind to suffer
    The slings and arrows of outrageous fortune,
    Or to take arms against a sea of troubles,
    And by opposing end them? To die—to sleep,
    No more; and by a sleep to say we end
    The heart-ache, and the thousand natural shocks
    That flesh is heir to: 'tis a consummation

Devoutly to be wish'd. To die, to sleep.
To sleep, perchance to dream.

(*Hamlet* 3.1.58–67)

This speech is built upon apposition: the juxtaposition, the rubbing together of word on word, phrase on phrase and idea upon idea. Observe how he juxtaposes not only single words and phrases, 'to be / not to be', 'to die / to sleep', but whole concepts:

Whether 'tis nobler in the mind to suffer
The slings and arrows of outrageous fortune

with

Or to take arms against a sea of troubles,
And by opposing end them?

The impact is twofold. Firstly it gives the actor and the director a really dynamic tool – 'to be or not to be' – the language wrestles with the thoughts. You can balance the words lightly, or you can positively chew them. Secondly it gives the actor, director and the audience an intellectual structure that allows us to explore the complex themes of life and death, suicide, our very existence.

Apposition is the single most important feature of Shakespeare's writing. Therefore, as you rehearse, don't be afraid to point out the antitheses and appositions to your actors. It will immediately make the language more muscular.

So **apposition** is key to an actor's methodology but also key to *a director's understanding of Shakespeare's* **dramaturgy**, both in terms of the structure of a speech as well as the shape and form of a whole play. His use of apposition creates **dramatic energy**. It was an idea that he lit upon early in his career and used constantly throughout his life. Jonson's way of writing is totally different, as is Marlowe's or Webster's.

Let's see how this works in practice. Here are some juxtapositions to look out for.

1. **Small scene, big scene.** Shakespeare frequently jumps from a scene with one, two or three characters to a scene involving large groups. In *Henry V*, after the Chorus, there follows a scene between two clerics, Canterbury and Ely; and then Bang! enter the entire English court. In the *Dream*, he starts with the full court and slims down, leaving just two lovers.

    This small scene/big scene structure was taken up in Europe in the nineteenth century especially by Schiller and Verdi, two of his great disciples. They both based their dramaturgy on Shakespeare's.

2. This can also happen *inside* a scene. Within the great ball scene in *R and J*, we cut away to Romeo and Juliet and hear their private conversation. This is the moment they first meet and fall in love; Shakespeare writes it in the form of a sonnet, a formal love poem. This 'cut away' gives special focus and energy to this crucial moment. It's theatrically brilliant as it demonstrates perfectly the way their obsessive love shuts out all surrounding action and noise. This section offers great opportunities to the director. Think of three or four ways you could exploit this or sharpen it.

3. **Public/private.** In many of his plays, but especially in the histories and the tragedies, Shakespeare shows us how characters operate in the public world and then reveals a whole different side of themselves in private. The private man/public face. This fascinated Shakespeare all his life. In *Henry V*, on the one hand we see the King surrounded by his army,

confident, charismatic, exhorting his troops to battle; on the other, we see him alone, praying, wracked with guilt that he gained the throne by illegitimate means. Throughout his work, Shakespeare connects private thoughts to great public events, the killing of a King or the division of a kingdom.

This technique allows the audience to have a 360-degree look at the character. It allows us to 'walk around' a character and examine him/her from different angles. It also offers a rounded, human perspective on history.

4   A **serious** scene followed by something **lighter, or funny**. The Porter in *Macbeth* offers a good example of this, or the Fool in *Lear*.

An understanding of this aspect of Shakespeare's dramaturgy will have important, practical implications for your production. How?

You will need to **design** a set that will allow you to move freely between a scene with twenty people onstage to one with just two. There are usually dozens of scenes in a Shakespeare play and if you have to move scenery between each one, you are dead in the water. Of course, Shakespeare didn't have this challenge; he wrote for an open stage with little or no scenery and, as already noted, the principal means of communication would be through the language.

In your work on the **staging**, you can really exploit these big/little, public/private juxtapositions. For example, you can make a hard, sharp cut, by creating movement and energy on the exit of, say, the court in the *Dream*, leaving the lovers suddenly alone. Or you can gradually 'leak' characters off the stage – a soft cut. They each mean something quite different.

You can create a dynamic **LX plot** that dramatizes these juxtapositions in the structure.

You can create a **style of movement** that helps focus the eye of the audience. For example the revellers at the ball in *R and J* could go into slo-mo while the lovers are meeting. Risky and some would regard as old hat. But your choice! Onwards!

Metaphor

I use this word to include metaphors, allusions, similes, classical references and flights of fancy. We touched on metaphor when considering how to address Shakespeare's world. I described metaphors as *the highway to the imagination*; they reveal essential aspects of each character, sometimes conscious, sometimes subconscious and, equally important, they act as stimuli to the audience's imagination.

Metaphor is a fuel to your actor's imagination and needs to be appreciated and ingested. Be ready to point out in rehearsal the use of metaphor as it may well be hidden. Your actors will find a treasure trove of clues to their character's inner life.

In Hamlet's speech above, he talks of

> The slings and arrows of outrageous fortune.

The metaphor communicates his frustration; but more than this, it reveals the extremity, the extravagance of his emotions. The actor needs to identify where this comes from and *embrace* it.
In the same speech he says

> Or to take arms against a sea of troubles.

The violent imagery continues but leads him into a nightmarish vision of 'a sea of troubles'. You can't fight a stormy sea with a sword. So on the one hand we have a speech that confronts the notion of suicide in a dynamic, quite rational way, using apposition to explore the arguments; on the other, the metaphors reveal a character wrestling with extreme emotions and nightmares.

My tip to the actor playing Hamlet would be to *coin* the metaphors, to invent them in the moment; let the character *search* for the right expression, as if he's making it up on the spot. That way, the image 'sea of troubles' almost pops out of the character's subconscious.

Metaphor constantly reveals a character's inner life or subconscious. Revisit the speech of Juliet I quoted earlier, beginning:

> JULIET
> Gallop apace, you fiery-footed steeds,
> Towards Phoebus' lodging: such a wagoner
> As Phaethon would whip you to the west,
> And bring in cloudy night immediately.
> Spread thy close curtain, love-performing night,
> That runaway's eyes may wink and Romeo
> Leap to these arms, untalk'd of and unseen.
>
> (*Romeo and Juliet* 3.2.1–7)

This whole speech is *dripping* with metaphor and betrays a passionate sexuality, a longing for darkness and, hidden in the metaphors, a close kinship with death. In many ways it is Juliet's *imagination* that marks her out as a tragic character as much as the cruel twists of fate. She reads juicy works of fiction, she self-dramatizes, she is on the very brink of sexual awakening, she is wilful. Her almost unbearable situation is expressed and explored in this metaphor laden speech. It's vital that your actor invents these metaphors and really connects with them imaginatively. A word of warning. The danger is that the speech becomes over-coloured and cloying. As the director you must monitor this; a colourful image is all the more powerful if set against more plain speech. This speech needs great technical skill as well as deep resources of emotion.

A metaphor is frequently passed on from one character to another. Make a note of where this happens. Here's an example from *R and J*, the sonnet in the ball scene.

ROMEO
[To JULIET] If I profane with my unworthiest hand
This holy shrine, the gentle sin is this:
My lips, two blushing pilgrims, ready stand
To smooth that rough touch with a tender kiss.

JULIET
Good pilgrim, you do wrong your hand too much,
Which mannerly devotion shows in this;
For saints have hands that pilgrims' hands do touch,
And palm to palm is holy palmers' kiss.

ROMEO
Have not saints lips, and holy palmers too?

JULIET
Ay, pilgrim, lips that they must use in prayer.

ROMEO
O, then, dear saint, let lips do what hands do;
They pray, grant thou, lest faith turn to despair.

JULIET
Saints do not move, though grant for prayers' sake.

ROMEO
Then move not, while my prayer's effect I take. (They kiss)
(*Romeo and Juliet* 1.4.93–106)

Here Romeo sets up the metaphor, her body as shrine, his lips as pilgrims. Juliet picks up the metaphor which they develop together and resolve with a kiss. A couple of things to note. The actors are reliant on each other to make the scene work: the metaphor has to be passed precisely from one to the other. It is a wooing scene, but a dangerous one; there is an inbuilt challenge in the dialogue. Can you match me? Do you have the wit? Can you keep this ball in the air? Can we make this really special? The metaphor defines their love; it is both sacred and sexual, flirtatious and deadly serious.

So look for *shared metaphors* and make a note.

Metre and Pulse

There are two aspects of rhythm that you should consider:

- The rhythm and pulse of the text, whether it be verse or prose
- The rhythm of the whole play.

Here's a line from the *Dream*:

LYSANDER
    I am, my lord, as well derived as he.
                                (*A Midsummer Night's Dream* 1.1.99)

Shakespeare used the iambic pentameter as his basic working tool throughout his life. It's not complicated; it has a pulse of five beats (pentameter) and an iambic rhythm (de dum de dum de dum de dum de dum). You can beat out the pulse with your hand on the table. The above line is a clearly stated opinion. It has strength in its rhythm.

Now let's look once more at the opening lines of *Henry V*.

CHORUS
> O for a Muse of fire, that would ascend
> The brightest heaven of invention,
> A kingdom for a stage, princes to act
> And monarchs to behold the swelling scene!
> Then should the warlike Harry, like himself,
> Assume the port of Mars; and at his heels,
> Leash'd in like hounds, should famine, sword and fire
> Crouch for employment.

There are some variations here. He starts with a strong beat 'O'. He uses another strong beat on the fifth line 'Then', and another on 'Leash'd'. These variations of rhythm give the actor power, command and dramatic thrust, a necessity, I would imagine in the Globe Theatre in the early seventeenth century when performing in the open air to an audience of thousands. Check the variations in your text before rehearsals; you might need to point them out to actors, the purpose being *empowerment*. I almost never use the words iambic pentameter in rehearsal. Actors must feel the pulse in their bones. Rehearsals are not an academic exercise. A sense of rhythm, a response to pulse is innate in all human beings; as a director you need to encourage the *harnessing* of these impulses in the language of the play. The key to this is to make the exploration of rhythm and pulse integral to your process and *fun*.

Occasionally, Shakespeare would use four beats to the line, sometimes three, even two and these variations would signal important dramatic departures. Look at the first scene of Puck and the First Fairy, a crazy, exhilarating beat, like a cantering horse:

PUCK
> How now, spirit! whither wander you?

FAIRY
> Over hill, over dale,
> Thorough bush, thorough brier,
> Over park, over pale,
> Thorough flood, thorough fire,
> I do wander everywhere,
> Swifter than the moon's sphere;
> And I serve the fairy queen,
> To dew her orbs upon the green.
>
> (*A Midsummer Night's Dream* 2.1.1–9)

If you get your actors to follow the rhythms and to celebrate the exuberance of the language, you will find a release of fun and wildness into the scene.

Of great importance to the director is **an appreciation of the rhythm of the play**. All works of art are possessed of rhythm, some obviously so, like a symphony or a jazz suite or a ballet, some less obviously so, like a painting or a sculpture.

A great play, whether it be by Shakespeare or Pinter or Wertenbaker will have rhythm. Try to get a deep sense of the rhythm of the play you are directing. This is partly a function of the great structural movements of the story, your beginning, middle and end, partly the juxtaposition of scenes and characters as described earlier. The regular intervention of the Chorus in *Henry V*, with his powerful rhythm gives this play a strong forward impulse, like an unputdownable novel. The potency and frequency of the monologues in the early acts of *Macbeth*, often spoken at night, create a claustrophobic, introspective atmosphere that opens out dramatically and unexpectedly in the latter movement of the play. This, by the way, can create a challenge in the performance of the last scenes, as I'll discuss when considering cuts in Chapter 9.

The balance of verse scenes with prose scenes will also contribute to the rhythm of the play. Prose scenes are invariably more naturalistic (although beware – prose has its own rhythms as well. The key with prose is to identify the appositions and really work them).

The *situations* of your characters will also help define the rhythm of your play. Remember, for the young lovers in the *Dream*, it's a matter of life or death and this gives the flight to the forest great forward impulse. Many, many of Shakespeare's characters are emotionally highly charged, almost super-charged and this will affect the forward thrust of the production. Always look for clues in the language that will act as pointers to the overall shape and try and keep these pointers handy in your back pocket as you progress through rehearsals. Actor *x* may want to play such and such a scene very slowly; you need to have a good sense where this scene fits into the play *rhythmically* to counter this if necessary.

Line Endings

Line endings in verse are a brilliant pointer to *how a character thinks*. They will often tell you, quite precisely, how thoughts are formed, developed and move forward. As such, they are invaluable to an actor who is striving to create a full inner life for a character.

I am *not* suggesting that you encourage your actors to take a pause at the end of each line and then proceed on to the next. This can sound very artificial and old fashioned. What I do say to my actors is that *they should play through to the end of the line*, but not necessarily 'end stop'. What I also say is that they can pause for as long as they like in a speech, as long as it's at the end of a line! Let's see how this works in practice.

Here's a speech by Henry V, exhorting his troops to make one last effort to conquer the fortress of Harfleur.

KING HENRY V
> Once more unto the breach, dear friends, once more;
> Or close the wall up with our English dead.
> In peace there's nothing so becomes a man
> As modest stillness and humility:
> But when the blast of war blows in our ears,
> Then imitate the action of the tiger;
> Stiffen the sinews, summon up the blood,
> Disguise fair nature with hard-favour'd rage;
> Then lend the eye a terrible aspect;
> Let pry through the portage of the head
> Like the brass cannon; let the brow o'erwhelm it
> As fearfully as doth a galled rock
> O'erhang and jutty his confounded base,
> Swill'd with the wild and wasteful ocean.
> Now set the teeth and stretch the nostril wide,
> Hold hard the breath and bend up every spirit
> To his full height. On, on, you noblest English.
> Whose blood is fet from fathers of war-proof!
> Fathers that, like so many Alexanders,
> Have in these parts from morn till even fought
> And sheathed their swords for lack of argument:
> Dishonour not your mothers; now attest
> That those whom you call'd fathers did beget you.
> Be copy now to men of grosser blood,
> And teach them how to war. And you, good yeoman,
> Whose limbs were made in England, show us here
> The mettle of your pasture; let us swear

> That you are worth your breeding; which I doubt not;
> For there is none of you so mean and base,
> That hath not noble lustre in your eyes.
> I see you stand like greyhounds in the slips,
> Straining upon the start. The game's afoot:
> Follow your spirit, and upon this charge
> Cry 'God for Harry, England, and Saint George!'
>
> (*King Henry V* 3.1.1–34)

The action of the speech is pretty clear: to persuade his troops, who have probably already taken a fair old battering, to make another super human exertion. It's a great speech to study because it shows all the hallmarks of fine public speaking; it is inspiring, detailed, specific and perfectly shaped to achieve its goal. What I want you to notice here is the way that, as the speech progresses, Shakespeare increasingly puts the full stop or semicolon in the middle of the line. Challenge yourself. No pauses in the middle of the line, only at the line ending. Look at this example:

> Hold hard the breath and bend up every spirit
> To his full height. On, on, you noblest English.

You could pause after 'height', take a breath and carry on. But try it another way. If you press on through the pentameter to the word 'English' with no break or pause, you get an immediate surge of energy, the speech quickens and Henry takes the thought right through to the patriotic word 'English'. Now, the first option tells us of a King who is focused and says the right thing; the second character is more dangerous, more of an improviser, quicker witted. Henry thinks in this way seven times during this speech, mostly in the second half of the speech. If you and your actor recognize this particular use of line ending, you will learn an immense amount about the character and his persuasive power. The speech will quicken and lead unstoppably to the mass exit at the end of the scene to storm the walls of Harfleur.

So in your prep, make a little note of whenever a character is written with full stops or colons in the middle of lines.

Word Play: Rhyme, Alliteration and Assonance

The operative word here is *play*.

Throughout his work, in comedy, in tragedy, history or romance, Shakespeare revelled in the sheer *fun* of words and word play, a facility that fascinates the mind and constantly lifts the spirit of the listener. The problem, and it's a big problem, is that his wizardry with words can often be seen as an obstacle or barrier to audience and performers alike. This is partly real and partly illusory.

It's real because, without question, Shakespeare's language is 'heightened' and will die in the mouth and fall flat on the ear of the listener if you try to make it simply conversational or, worse still, gimmicky. It's illusory because when your actors embrace the language and stop trying to 'translate' it into a twenty-first-century patois, then it will communicate brilliantly. I know this from considerable firsthand experience. My office at Stratford was situated near the back of the auditorium and, most days, I would slip in and watch a bit of whatever show was playing. The stalls (orchestra) was invariably populated by large groups of school kids who were clearly enthralled. One afternoon, after a performance of *Hamlet* that I directed at Stratford Ontario, I was confronted by a huge group of teenagers waiting for their bus to take them over the border to Detroit. They were delighted (as was I), and clearly had no problem with the language.

So embrace the challenge and get your actors to *relish* the language.

Here's the speech from the *Dream* in which Hermia commits to eloping with Lysander.

HERMIA
>My good Lysander!
>I swear to thee, by Cupid's strongest bow,
>By his best arrow with the golden head,
>By the simplicity of Venus' doves,
>By that which knitteth souls and prospers loves,
>And by that fire which burn'd the Carthage queen,
>When the false Troyan under sail was seen,
>By all the vows that ever men have broke,
>In number more than ever women spoke,
>In that same place thou hast appointed me,
>To-morrow truly will I meet with thee.
>
>>(*A Midsummer Night's Dream* 1.1.168–178)

This is wonderfully extravagant and over the top and perfectly captures her teenage enthusiasm and spontaneity. She grabs a whole handful of classical allusions to help her and reinforce her commitment to his wild idea. But what else? Look at the line endings. On the fourth and fifth lines she makes a rhyme ('doves' and 'loves') and then stays in rhyme for the rest of the speech. These rhymes underline her certainty; they are a verbal handshake. Furthermore, they are fun and open the door to a great adventure in the forest. I think you should get your actor to invent the rhyme *quite consciously*. As the character he/she should be thinking 'What rhymes with doves', etc. In this way, language becomes part of their relationship, part of their love.

You will find that in the rest of this play, there are hundreds and hundreds of rhymes; each one should be invented and captured. This way a style of communication with the audience will develop and, crucially, it will prevent your actors from dropping the ends of their lines. This is a classic mistake with young actors and one that is certain to send your audience into a deep sleep.

So take a highlighter pen and go through a copy of the script and mark up all the rhymes, alliterations, assonances, anything that is characterful and quirky. I promise that you and your actors will find this a revelation.

Vocabulary

The vocabulary used by Shakespeare is vast. We know that London at the time was a melting pot of Elizabethan/Jacobean society and we know that all classes, rich and poor, educated and illiterate, townsfolk and country people crammed into the Globe to hear the plays. They would have carried with them their local dialect, vocabulary and accent. It is highly likely that the diversity of regional accents was stronger and richer than today and that Shakespeare himself would have had a marked Warwickshire accent. There is little evidence in the plays of the accent snobbery that still blights our class-ridden UK society. In *Love's Labour's Lost* the highly educated pedants Sir Nathaniel and Holofernes feel mightily superior to the constable Dull. Their vocabulary is considerable and littered with classical allusions; Dull has a much smaller vocabulary and misunderstands their meanings, but has a simple rural charm that outshines his companions.

As you prepare your production take account of the vocabulary used by the characters as this will help create the world in which they exist. And at this point you might consider whether to use regional accents.

Look at these opening lines from *Romeo and Juliet*:

SCENE 1. Verona. A public place.

Enter **SAMPSON** *and* **GREGORY**, *of the house of Capulet*

> SAMPSON Gregory, o' my word, we'll not carry coals.
> GREGORY No, for then we should be colliers.
> SAMPSON I mean, an we be in choler, we'll draw.
> GREGORY Ay, while you live, draw your neck out o' the collar.
> SAMPSON I strike quickly, being moved.
> GREGORY But thou art not quickly moved to strike.
> SAMPSON A dog of the house of Montague moves me.
> GREGORY To move is to stir; and to be valiant is to stand: therefore, if thou art moved, thou runn'st away.
> SAMPSON A dog of that house shall move me to stand: I will take the wall of any man or maid of Montague's.
> GREGORY That shows thee a weak slave; for the weakest goes to the wall.
> SAMPSON True; and therefore women, being the weaker vessels, are ever thrust to the wall: therefore I will push Montague's men from the wall, and thrust his maids to the wall.
> GREGORY The quarrel is between our masters and us their men.
> SAMPSON 'Tis all one, I will show myself a tyrant: when I have fought with the men, I will be cruel with the maids, and cut off their heads.
> GREGORY The heads of the maids?

SAMPSON Ay, the heads of the maids, or their maidenheads;
take it in what sense thou wilt.
GREGORY They must take it in sense that feel it.
SAMPSON Me they shall feel while I am able to stand: and
'tis known I am a pretty piece of flesh.
GREGORY 'Tis well thou art not fish; if thou hadst, thou hadst been
poor John. Draw thy tool! here comes two of the house of the
Montagues.
SAMPSON My naked weapon is out: quarrel, I will back thee.

(*Romeo and Juliet* 1.1.1–33)

This is street talk. It's full of macho swagger and sexual innuendo. It's a private world that Shakespeare allows us to tune into. It's fascinating because it is full of word play and pun. Their world is created not just by the vocabulary, but by the rhythm. They know each other well and use language to egg each other on to violence. The situation on the street corner is vivid and contemporary. The vocabulary is not esoteric but the language has a 'heightened' quality to it, telling us much about these preening young men. Think about how you might help the two actors playing these parts. They can be totally recognizable to a modern audience but must wear the language like a vividly coloured costume. It's not 'chat' and cannot be thrown away. It has to be 'presented', even served up. Antony Burgess caught this cadence in his novel *A Clockwork Orange*, as did Kubrick in the film thereof.

Compare this to the Juliet speech quoted on page 51. She is clearly much better educated, has a much more sophisticated vocabulary and range of literary and classical references. These reflect the complexity of her emotions and the complication of her situation. The speech is driven by a whole series of active verbs: *gallop, whip, spread, leap, come, hood, come, come, come, come.* She accurately describes herself as an 'impatient child'.

And keep an eye out for *monosyllabic lines*. Slow them up so that you can fulfil all the vowel sounds. Vowels need space.

Vowels carry the emotion, consonants carry the thought

Shape and Structure

In my book *How to do Shakespeare*, I wrote this:

> Every speech tells a story.
> Every speech has a beginning, a middle and an end.
> Every speech starts with a headline.

And this:

> Every speech or section of dialogue tells a story.
> Every speech or section of dialogue has a beginning, a middle and an end.
> Every speech or section of dialogue starts with a headline.

Shakespeare was peerless in his understanding of the art of storytelling. He knows how to alert the audience, grab their attention and follow through with a narrative. Storytelling is central to the director's craft, in theatre and in film. How do you *make* the audience listen? How do you get the audience to watch what you want them to watch? How do you engage their emotions? The sections on staging and music will partly answer these questions, but here we'll focus on how he told stories with words and how you can help your actors deliver those stories. Here's a speech by the King of France in *Henry V*. He exhorts his noblemen to battle.

KING OF FRANCE
Where is Montjoy the herald? speed him hence: 36
Let him greet England with our sharp defiance.

> Up, princes! and, with spirit of honour edged
> More sharper than your swords, hie to the field:
> Charles Delabreth, high constable of France;   40
> You Dukes of Orleans, Bourbon, and of Berri,
> Alencon, Brabant, Bar, and Burgundy;
> Jaques Chatillon, Rambures, Vaudemont,
> Beaumont, Grandpre, Roussi, and Fauconberg,
> Foix, Lestrale, Bouciqualt, and Charolois;   45
> High dukes, great princes, barons, lords and knights,
> For your great seats now quit you of great shames.
> Bar Harry England, that sweeps through our land
> With pennons painted in the blood of Harfleur:
> Rush on his host, as doth the melted snow.   50
> Upon the valleys, whose low vassal seat
> The Alps doth spit and void his rheum upon:
> Go down upon him, you have power enough,
> And in a captive chariot into Rouen
> Bring him our prisoner.
>
> (*King Henry V* 3.5.36–55)

This speech tells a wonderful story. Its function is to conjure the might of the French army and thus create jeopardy for the English hero, Henry. It's done entirely through words. The speech has a *headline*, I would suggest 'sharp defiance'. This is bold and vivid and creates a strong launch. It has a *beginning*, he calls for Montjoy in the first two lines; a *middle*, he summons the great noblemen of France from lines 38 to 47; and an *end*, he describes how he wants the battle to conclude. This structure gives the actor a framework. Within the structure you can tease out ideas crucial to your production. For example, he introduces the idea of honour at the beginning of the middle section; honour, an idea that has been used through the ages to inspire young men to fight, or to point them on the road to their deaths. What interpretation does your production give to this? You may consider cutting the list of French noblemen; but pause, try saying the names out loud. You will find that the very sound of the names conjures the power of a great civilization. And, of course, it's highly unlikely that your production will boast so many actors; the list works for you on the audience's imagination. Finally he chucks in a mighty metaphor of the snow melting from the Alps, leaving us in no two minds that Henry and the English have a great battle on their hands.

Challenge yourself: take any speech from any Shakespeare play and do the above exercise.

As a follow up, take a short scene from any play and try the same exercise.

You will sometimes find that a particular scene is not firing properly. The lines are in the right order but there is no energy. This analysis will help you. Storytelling in theatre is both an individual and a collective responsibility. You might ask the actor playing the French King, does this speech live up to its headline? Does it inspire 'sharp defiance'? Perhaps the action of the King needs to be sharpened. Perhaps the reaction of his fellows onstage needs to be stronger. Does the scene deliver its purpose, to create jeopardy for the English army? It's a collective responsibility. You might also find that it helps to have titles for each section of a scene. These can be evocative and inspirational. Take, for example, the opening scene of *Romeo and Juliet* which begins with the scene examined above. Take it as far as Romeo's entrance. You might call the beginning, the section printed above, ' Peacocks'. You might call the middle section, the fights, the 'Ruck' and you might call the final section when the Prince arrives, 'Judgement'.

Another exercise I sometimes use to focus minds is to pose the hypothetical question: 'I'm going to cut every line in this speech bar one. Which line do you keep?' Try it on the French King's speech. You might choose 'sharp defiance' but you might also choose 'Bring him our prisoner'. I'm in favour of the latter because it encourages the actor to play the speech building towards the last words, a hidden crescendo if you like. It's a common error of inexperienced actors to finish their speeches with a weak ending. Finish strongly, or at the least firmly, and you will hand over the baton to the next actor who takes it up and moves the story forward.

Back to our narrative. Let's design the show.

5

Let's Design It! The Eye

Now you have a strong sense of the structure of the play, *the journey of the play*, let's design it.

Your Designer

The **relationship** with your designer is key to the fulfilment of your production. In most cases, the designer will be the first person with whom you will engage in discussion about the play, the first person upon whom you will try out your ideas.

If you are lucky, you will have developed a relationship or friendship with a designer. This is the perfect situation and it puts you right round the track. But you may find you have to go and search for someone, or perhaps the theatre management might stipulate that you must work with x or y.

In my career, I have been in all three situations. When I started at the Bristol Old Vic, the brilliant designer Bob Crowley was starting there at exactly the same time. We subsequently worked together for the next twenty years. But at Bristol, I also had to work with their 'house' designers, and subsequently I have had to seek out new relationships. In most cases these situations have worked out very well and I count these colleagues as close friends.

Your designer is your first collaborator, so choose carefully. Follow your instinct, research possible candidates as thoroughly as possible. In Britain, the National Theatre hosts a terrific annual exhibition of the work of young designers, the Linbury Prize. If you are a student, you will find that these designers are exactly the same age as you and will likely be looking to form creative relationships just like you. Most designers these days have splendid websites, but also try and see their work 'live', in a theatre if possible. Do you like their work, would you trust their taste? Don't be shy to ask to meet face to face 'without prejudice'. You'll want to get a feeling for the chemistry between you, but also you'll need to get an idea of their working methods. Are they flexible in their approach? Will they challenge you (*good*)? Will they inspire you (*better*)?

Now you have a collaborator, a colleague and, hopefully, a friend.

As you work with your designer, always try to approach the play in a visual way. Many of us, myself included, have an academic background. We may have taken a degree in English Literature or the humanities. Having a sharp intellect and good analytic skills are important, but as a director, they will only get you so far. Actors rarely approach their work from an intellectual point of view and designers almost never, even though they are often super bright.

Despite all the preparatory work you have done, **avoid entering the design process with a completely fixed idea** of what you want your show to look like. Of course, it sometimes happens that you have a totally clear, brilliant idea of the world, the production, the whole concept. 'I'm going to do 12th Night set on a yacht in the Mediterranean.' That's totally fine.

As a director, always think of yourself as a *traveller* **open to real collaborations** as more and more colleagues join your journey. The designer, the actors, the lighting designer, the composer, all of your technical team and, finally, the audience. This way of thinking will certainly enrich the work, but will also make the process much more satisfactory for your team.

So how to work with your designer?

To Start

To start with, try these four steps:

1 **Create a wall of ideas**
2 **Read the play out loud**
3 **Analyse and discuss**
4 **Brainstorm**

Wall of ideas

Some designers **create a whole wall** of photographs, newspaper articles, drawings, cartoons, images off the net. Sometimes this is created digitally on one of the many platforms available.

Put on your 'wall' anything that resonated about the play, even if you don't fully appreciate its significance at this stage. You must follow your instincts. For example, when I was preparing Handel's *Alcina* for the Vienna Staatsoper, Antony Ward, the designer, showed me an image of a hot-air balloon landing in a rather grand drawing room. We kept returning to it over the coming weeks and eventually it provided the key to the whole *mise en scène*.

Read out loud

I have always found it highly beneficial to **read the whole play out loud** with the designer, reading alternate speeches or divying up the parts as you go along. Stop and start as and when you want. Discuss. You will probably learn some interesting things for yourself and you will certainly receive new thoughts from your designer.

Analyse and discuss

Sooner or later you should **present some or all of your analysis** to your designer. Tell him/her about the structure, about the three movements, describe the world of the play, talk about the characters and try to define what, to you, the play is about. Sometimes I will communicate this in written form, but most often I will present my ideas face to face; sometimes all at once, sometimes piecemeal, after each act or movement. If you have any visual images, share them, stick them on the wall. You will immediately start getting feedback and the dialogue begins!

Have a full discussion about the world of the play. Find imagery. This need not be a literal response. You may be seeking imagery for 'patriarchal' or 'claustrophobic'. You may find a photo of a child in an alley or a pair of old shoes. Stick it on the wall. Some directors and designers find that the work of a painter or photographer is particularly inspiring and, indeed, you could create an entire production with the look of a Hopper painting or a Hammershoi interior. Such a choice can be highly illuminating, indeed revelatory. Perhaps you identify a 'parallel culture' to that of the play – a Japanese Samurai military world for example. This has not often been my approach; I have usually preferred to follow my imagination into different realms. But if, for example, the work of Don McCullin, the celebrated war photographer, gives you a way into *Henry V*, then trust this, follow it through.

Brainstorm

Allow plenty of time for a good, no-holds-barred, no limits, general, wide-ranging discussion about the play. Brainstorm!

Questions you might ask include:

- What is the most powerful image in the play?
- When our audience leave the theatre, how do we want them to feel?
- What discussion would we like to provoke?
- Do we find some of it boring? Inexplicable?
- Which character do we most empathize with?
- Why do we want to present this play?
- What contemporary relevance does it have?
- What aspect is particularly *theatrical* and perfectly suited to this medium?
- What is personal to you about this play?
- Is there a particular moment or event that will predicate the whole production?
- What are the elements of the play? Earth, fire air or water?

The brainstorm discussion is a vital stage in the development of any production. You will need to trust your designer and respect him/her. It's the stage in which your joint imagination must have full rein. Continue the process of **collecting images** – visual responses to the story.

The Model

Next comes the **model stage**, for me the most exciting part of the design process.

I would strongly encourage you to **work in 3D in a model box**. This requires the designer or the theatre management to supply a 'to scale' model of the stage where your production will take place. This may be huge and grand like the Olivier Theatre or a small 'black box'. It can be scaled 1:25, or 1:50. It doesn't matter; it's your intellectual and emotional playground during the design process.

Nowadays, technology allows us to create a **virtual model** of the set, exactly to scale, with virtual actors that you can move around. You can see the stage from every seat in the house and every corner of the auditorium from every position onstage.

I have worked in both situations and, under no circumstances would I again work digitally. Why?

Paradoxically, I found the digital experience a great limitation on my imagination. However wonderful, I was still looking at pictures rather than spaces. I found that I was constantly being shown 'found' material, i.e. images grabbed from other sources, rather than directly out of the designer's imagination. And the process was less collaborative, as only the designer could move around the 'pieces', the walls or the actors.

This is an ongoing debate and you and your designer will certainly come to a view on this. I will proceed with the 3D model system that I have found most creative.

Let's start off in a **proscenium theatre**, by which I mean any theatre with a stage at one end and the audience at the other. This can be a village hall, a converted lecture theatre or an architectural masterpiece created by Frank Matcham, the great Victorian/Edwardian theatre designer. I call them 'two-room' theatres; the audience in one room looking at the actors in another. (We'll look at thrust stages and theatre in the round a little later in this chapter.)

A Methodology

The following methodology of work applies to *all* shapes and sizes of theatre and all texts, ancient or modern.

Ok, so we have a scale model of the stage. This is usually painted black and into it you will place pieces of white card or paper with which you will be able to develop your ideas. You will be able to work quite quickly and cheaply. Don't worry about colour or decoration at this stage.

Space

First consider the **space** of the play.

With space, you need to think **technically and emotionally**.
With space, you need to think **subjectively and objectively**.

Quick detour: search on Google for an image of Leonardo da Vinci's 'Vitruvian Man' (1490). This is the image of a naked man standing in a circle with his arms outstretched and his legs in two positions, together and apart. Now, imagine yourself as that creature, looking outwards. Imagine energy streaming out of your four limbs. You are creating space in three dimensions. This is what the actor does when he stands onstage. He projects space; he creates space through his energy and his thought. He's a magician. Now flip the camera and look at the man objectively. As a director, you have to do both.

Get into the habit of thinking '3D'. As with your Vitruvian Man, there is space above the actor and below the actor, to his left and to her right, before and behind. **Think of the stage, like Shakespeare's Globe Theatre, as a complete universe.** There is Man/Woman standing on the stage, the earth; there is space above, some would call this the 'heavens' or the 'gods' or the sky; and space below the surface of the stage, in Medieval times, Hell, a dark and dangerous place; for us now, more interesting, less morally prescriptive.

Bear this in mind as you explore the space of the play. **Use the whole stage to create a complete cosmos.** For the Ancients, the gods would have descended from above; where would you place an entrance for a god nowadays? Through the audience, surely. If you are working on a Shakespeare play, there will certainly be a strong spiritual dimension. This may be explicit as in the *Dream* with a whole host of 'Immortals' and a huge invisible world; or implicit as with *R and J*, where death and the afterlife closely stalk the protagonists and their actions carry a heavy moral burden. **Your stage is the universe of the play** and here, your reading of the world of the play is vital. Is there a moral force in the play or is the universe desolate and mankind alone? You can take a materialist view of the play and offer a critique of Shakespeare's world. But think big; it's a whole world. Are there any images that express your feelings about this universe or cosmos? Put them on the wall.

Let's stick with Vitruvian Man for one more second. There is a **time** element. He looks ahead, into the future. Behind him is the past. An actor will use space quite instinctively and refer behind him to things past and in front when he talks of the future. Be aware of this as you explore the space of your production.

Now let's tackle the basics.

The mechanics: Floors

Take your analysis of big scene/little scene. Don't worry about how a scene might be decorated. Don't worry about period or style. That's for later. Think spatially.

First and obviously, ask yourself which scene or moment requires the largest, most epic space. How many characters do I need to fit onto the stage and what sort of interaction might they need? What about the monologues or 'two-handers'? Experiment with pieces of card of differing sizes representing the floor. You don't have to come to any conclusions yet, just start to learn the space.

Now think emotionally (yes, it's possible!). It will not always follow that a scene with a small group of characters requires a small space. Lear and the Fool on the heath is best played, in my opinion, on a very open stage. This choice will make them more vulnerable, more lonely, and it will make the elements more threatening.

Ask yourself, how do I best express the feelings that Romeo might experience while in exile in Mantua? Do I want a large space or confined? Find an image. As an exercise, try to imagine the space from inside the character's head. The architecture of a real backstreet in Mantua is less important than what it feels like to Romeo. Here, **design is subjective not objective**.

With the opening court scene of Hamlet, do you create the space *objectively* (i.e. what such a royal palace might actually look like) or *subjectively* (i.e. what it looks like from Hamlet's point of view)?

Both are valid. The latter is more expressionistic and perhaps takes us deeper into the heart of the play. This can, of course, lead to extreme interpretations. For example, you may think that Hamlet's view of the world is skewed by grief, so you create a space that is tilted at

45 degrees. Very hard to act on, especially for the other characters who don't share Hamlet's world view. Or he feels claustrophobic – so everyone is in a tiny room. Interesting but challenging.

The question here is: do I create a design, and therefore a point of view of the play, seen from one character's angle, or from multiple angles? For me, Shakespeare's humanism and the way he conceives of character lead me to the latter rather than the former. Shakespeare makes it hard for us to apply simple judgements on characters and situations. Macbeth speaks some of the most beautiful poetry in the English language; his thoughts are fine, even exquisite. However, he kills children.

One final point: actors have to work on the floor so make sure it's not dangerous or too uncomfortable!

The mechanics: Entrances and exits

Let us examine the mechanics of the play, the traffic of the play from *the actor's point of view*. Look at the **entrances and the exits**. And look at the axes of the play. I often refer to the entrances and exits as **doors**, even if no physical manifestation is required.

The theatre you are working in, or the space you have chosen, may well offer you multiple possibilities. Many newly built playhouses have a degree of flexibility undreamed of by the old Victorian theatre designers. This is true of many theatres on university campuses. Or you may be directing in the open air with the audience gathered around a large carpet; entrances can be made wherever you like. But it's highly instructive to analyse and boil down your choices to **what is needed to tell the story**.

Let's take an example from the *Dream*.

PUCK
> But, room, fairy! here comes Oberon.

FAIRY
> And here my mistress. Would that he were gone!
> (*A Midsummer Night's Dream* 2.i.58–59)

Enter Titania and Oberon who have a mighty row. So we need two 'doors', spaced well apart to create a powerful confrontation. This, of course, was readily available in Shakespeare's theatre.

In comedy, the positioning of the doors or entrances is of fundamental importance. Indeed, if you are directing a farce and you put the doors in the wrong place, you're sunk. The actors haven't got a chance; you won't get the laughs; the mechanics won't work.

The confrontation between Titania and Oberon needs to be instantaneous and direct. In my production for the RSC and the subsequent film, I punctured the set with doors, thereby offering quick and surprising entrances and exits, especially useful in the middle scenes when the four lovers keep bumping into and falling in love with, the 'wrong' boy/girl. I even placed doors beneath the stage which magically rose and fell, thereby solving many of the 'supernatural' challenges of the play. Of course, I had the resources of a national company at my disposal, but a similar effect could be achieved by having three or four free-standing door frames, moved around by the fairies, or even the lovers themselves. That would be a 'rough magic' solution which can often be the most stimulating and effective.

How about the opening scene of *Henry V*? Does the king need a special entrance? Possibly. This will give him status and empower the actor. The subject of the scene is power; the power to go to war, to put people's lives in danger. Does it need to be upstage centre? That's the traditional position and for very good reason. It will instantaneously solve many of the challenges of blocking (the placing and movement of characters onstage). Because the world of the play is so hierarchical, as already noted, the actors will have a pretty clear idea where they would stand and move in relation to the king.

For some scenes, the position of entrances and exits is of little importance; it can be worked out in rehearsal. But if you want a real challenge, work out the number and position of the doors in Act 2 of Mozart's *Marriage of Figaro*, the Countess's bedroom. It's a mind bender!

The mechanics: Axes

Make a note as well of the axes of different scenes.

It's likely that Shakespeare imagined that the mechanics of the Titania/Oberon scene are left to right, in width across the stage. That is the axis of the scene. The axis of the 'tennis ball' scene in *Henry V* is taken from the entrance of the king (Figure 1). Draw these axes and experiment with shifting them. Cut out a long strip of white card and use match boxes as doors. This will help you enormously when staging the play.

I have come to believe that there is such a thing as a tragic axis. I have directed all of Shakespeare's tragedies, some more than once, and quite a few Greek plays as well. Underpinning these plays is an energy, an inevitability if you like, that leads the characters and the audience inexorably towards death. It comes towards you, sometimes slowly, sometimes quickly, like a moving train. There is a ceremony being enacted here. I have learnt to reflect that in my designs. The

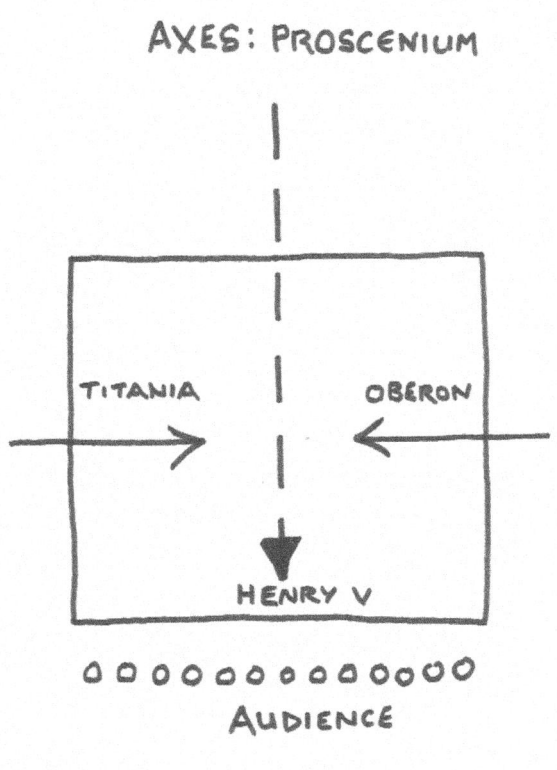

Figure 1 *Axes: proscenium. Drawing courtesy of Adrian Noble.*

actors I have worked with – Michael Gambon, Helen Mirren, Derek Jacobi, Robert Stephens, Ken Branagh – all know where they need to stand in order to deliver the part. In the same way, the great soprano Anna Netrebko knows where she needs to be in order to sing those hugely demanding roles.

The mechanics: Walls

By 'walls' I mean any membrane that obscures the audience's sightline on the stage; they may be made of canvass, plastic, wood or any of the materials that are available; they may be translucent, transparent or opaque.

An obvious, rather prosaic function of 'walls' is to prevent the audience from seeing right through to the back wall of the stage which may be rather unattractive or distracting. Similarly you may want to mask off the sides where you might see actors preparing for their entrance.

But in design, I always start with a full open stage which I find rather beautiful. In fact I have often opened the stage right up to the back. There is an honesty and directness about placing your action in an empty theatre; the focus falls firmly on the actor and the text. But be aware, there are acoustic implications of having an 'open' stage. You might consider having the actors onstage throughout the action, sitting, standing and watching.

Experiment with 'walls' *after* you have thought about the floor and entrances. If you have the budget, you may want to try a cyclorama, a stretched membrane the encloses the upstage area, either in a straight line or a curve. This has the benefit of providing a surface that can be lit with different colours and effects, or take projection. You can thus change the mood of the story, scene by scene.

If you have a flying facility, or can use trucks that can move scenery on from the wings, experiment with how this may change the space. A wall behind a character has a powerful effect, and can instantly turn an epic scene into a domestic scene. But this can also be achieved with simpler means; a mobile screen, a hatstand or even a few actors standing behind the action with their backs to the audience.

Be certain; you don't need to spend a large amount of money to create an imaginative, powerful show.

The skeleton

An important tip: try to design the skeleton of the play, its inner shape and not the outward form.

When I'm preparing a new show, I write out those words and stick them on the wall above my desk! Remember, your design must complement the text, rather than smother it; it must energize the story rather than illustrate it; it must support and enable the actor, rather than hinder. Think of it like this: your design should be *incomplete* until an actor steps on it.

This approach is particularly important when designing a Shakespeare play, or almost any classic. We have observed that Shakespeare's world is essentially a non-scenic space; his world was created by the words. If you try to follow the scenic indications *literally*, you might well get into trouble.

Here's an example. In *As You Like It*, Rosalind, Celia and Touchstone go into exile in the Forest of Arden. Now how do I design that? What sort of forest is it? What's the evidence? Well, in this forest you can run about freely ('Run, run, Orlando!'). We learn that Oliver is wounded by a lion. Rosalind refers to 'coneys', or rabbits. This is, of course, ecologically impossible. Lions and rabbits in the same forest? No way!

Shakespeare has created a forest of the imagination. He has created a plastic space that can evolve as fast as the audience's imagination. Now it's a nice friendly place with rabbits hopping around; now it's dangerous with hungry lions. We can, perhaps, recognize this environment from the children's stories of *Rupert the Bear* or the landscape of Tolkien's *Hobbit*.

As a director, you are working over four hundred years after Shakespeare. We have moved from the Wooden O, where the actor is silhouetted against his fellow creatures, through the two-room theatres where the actor is seen against artificial, painted scenery and arrived at a time in theatrical history when we are consciously trying to rediscover the 'one-room' experience known to Shakespeare. These might be 'courtyard' theatres, thrust stages or black boxes. There has never been a better time to create imaginative design that supports and complements the text, that projects and empowers the actor.

Another tip: try to design the *journey* of the play.

This means that you should try to mark the moments when your story shifts from one movement to another. In *As You Like It*, you might want to mark the arrival of Rosalind and Celia in the frozen forest, if, for you, that is significant. I will illustrate this notion with two 'casebooks' from my own work.

The Journey of the Play: Two Casebooks

Where possible, I try to conceive a design as a **developing sculpture** that evolves according to the action of the play. This is high risk but a very exciting path to follow.

King Lear describes the disintegration of a kingdom because of one man's foolish actions. I have directed the play three times: twice on the main stage in Stratford-upon-Avon and once at the Old Globe in San Diego. My interpretations have developed and, I hope, matured but my point of departure has remained the same. I imagine the stage as the land, as England. The action of the play corrupts, disfigures and destroys the land. I had envisioned the play in three movements. The first, the crisis, took me up to the entrance of Edgar as Mad

Tom, which is the moment that the King loses his sanity. The second movement, the chaos, describes the escalating violence in the land, culminating in the blinding of Gloucester. This is where I took the interval. My final movement began with the expulsion of Gloucester and the journey to Dover Beach.

In 1982 with Michael Gambon, I played the first movement on an open stage with a throne, a bench and a table and chairs. As Poor Tom, Edgar erupted out of the stage from below, forming a jagged hole, scattering floor boards everywhere. This hole was further excavated by the actors and became the hovel. During the interval we further excavated the stage, pulling up floorboards across the whole width, revealing a sandy covering and a tank of water at the very front edge.

In 1991 with Robert Stephens, I used the same visual narrative, minus the water, but developed the opening movement by starting the play with the whole stage covered with thick paper. Upon this paper, the Fool drew a crude map of England. As Lear made his division, the map was redrawn before everyone's eyes. Towards the end of the opening scene, the Fool ripped it apart as a dramatic critique of the King's foolish actions. The ripped paper added to the chaos at Edgar's spectacular entrance.

In 2010 with Bob Foxworth, I lost the paper but added a covering of leaves across the whole stage. I created a pier, running up and down stage centre, which gave me useful height for Lear in the opening scene, and more structure for Edgar to destroy. In the interval, we swept the leaves upstage and thus created a foreshore. In all three versions, the stage developed organically with the action.

Another example. I imagined **Macbeth** as a psychological thriller with the action unfolding in relation to the development of his mental state. With my designer, Bob Crowley, we created a black box, including a black translucent ceiling. As his paranoia increased, the walls quite literally closed in on him. Paradoxically, the black box offered us enormous artistic opportunities. For example, the fingers of a stairway slid from out the back wall, creating an unforgettable pathway to Duncan's death chamber. I'd imagined Lady Macbeth killing herself by throwing herself off the battlements, so, in her sleepwalking scene, I had a single plank shoot out of the floor downstage in front of her. She walked along it, out towards the front row of the audience. It was crazy but highly evocative of her emotional state.

In Verdi's opera of *Macbeth*, there is a grand banquet at which the ghost of Banquo appears. In New York I used a long, shaped, white sheet stretched by lengths of elastic to create the illusion of a magnificent table the width of the whole stage that could disappear instantly when one end was released. I used many chairs to create the image of a celebratory feast; these chairs could be moved to different parts of the stage as the action required. When Macbeth sees the ghost and reacts violently, the formal arrangements became wrecked. I left these chairs in disarray onstage and used them as the setting for the witches coven when he sees more visions. The same chairs were used by Lady Macbeth in the sleepwalking scene. I wanted a similar effect to my 'shooting plank' in Stratford, so through the long introduction to her sleepwalking aria, I got Anna Netrebko to walk downstage on one chair, then another, then another, the chairs being moved into place at the very last moment by three of the witches. So one idea organically developed into a design narrative.

Playtime

Put into your model a scale figure of an actor. This can be a cut-out piece of cardboard with a simple supporting structure on the back, or a real to-scale maquette, bought quite cheaply at an artist's model shop.

Choose a moment in the play. Not just any moment, but a moment that is key to the journey of the play. Perhaps King Henry on the night before Agincourt.

Now *play*!

Add a **floor**, square or round or wide and narrow, jagged at the edges. How does it feel? Work empirically. Trial and error. Does the floor feel right for the situation? What is the King experiencing at this moment in the play? Loneliness, I would imagine, self-doubt, vulnerability. What is the best floor to express this? A lone figure on a big empty space perhaps? Or on a narrow strip of floor, left to right, or diagonally, or up and down. Remember, if any such situation resonates, you can often recreate it with lighting. A lone figure lit from the side by a strong white light. By the way, you don't need an expensive lighting rig to create that effect; a couple of Maglites, one on either side, held by the actors would do the trick. I used this idea at the end of part one of *Hamlet* at Stratford Ontario, to great effect.

Don't get stuck. Refer back to your three movements and try another moment. Work on Hermia and Lysander's first entrance into the forest in the *Dream*. Think about **axis and entrance**. *Imagine* yourself into their situation. It's night time in a very scary place. You need to *conduct* the audience into their situation so they experience the fear, the loneliness along with the characters. The best way to do this is to create a moment of arrival, an entrance. This might be upstage centre between two very tall walls, thus exaggerating the vulnerability of the two young people, sandwiched between them. They might then walk downstage, carrying their belongings. There you have the beginnings of a staging. Again, this idea can also be shaped by the judicious use of light. I used a similar effect for the first entrance of the puppet in Kate Bush's stage show '*Before the Dawn*'; a pair of gigantic tall doors that slowly opened and the creature entered, heavily back lit.

I'm sure that **in the early stages of design, less is more**. Two characters with their suitcases standing in a 'corridor' of light, or on a strip of white card. Beautiful!

Does this simple image do more to conjure a wood at night than a more literal representation? **My instinct is to focus on the metaphorical implications of a forest** rather than lumbering yourself with a load of timber. We're creating a journey into chaos, in this case a wood outside Athens. So let's examine our options. Do I need trees? What kind of trees? How can I do this on a limited budget? Real trees, or scenery made to look like trees, flying in from the rig, could look wonderful. Can I *represent* trees in any way and does this help? You can consider painting trees on the backcloth, a method used happily for centuries. But is it you? Do you feel comfortable? I used giant lightbulbs suspended on wires that could swing, hover or create a 'jungle'.

You could consider *projecting* the forest. This can be highly effective and the forest can change character and mood, from dark to light, from sinister to welcoming, indeed from continent to continent, as the story unfolds. You can have a series of fixed images, a changing sequence or a full video. Projection has become a major piece of kit in the designer's tool box. Most experienced designers will tell you that it's very easy to overdo projection or to rely too heavily on it. (Remember, it *eats* up time in technical rehearsals!) There are now many specialist video practitioners. I have used video a lot, usually in combination with other design elements. Video can give you arresting, even shocking images that can complement your production. An obvious example would be to use images of the trenches in the First World War to conjure the battle of Agincourt in *Henry V*. A word of caution: in a way, you are *borrowing* an audience's reaction to the horror of a particular war to enhance your story. I don't think this is a moral issue; it's more that you are illustrating Shakespeare's text rather than engaging the audience directly with the words.

You can also use a **live camera** to enhance or even comment upon stage action. You can project a huge image of Henry's face on a screen as the actor delivers the speech at the siege of Harfleur. Very showy, but ask yourself, what do you want the audience to look at? Such a technique could, however, be amazing when Puck is tricking the Lovers or terrorizing the Mechanicals. Here, the medium is the magic and magic is the subject. Be rigorous!

Before you go whole heartedly down the projection route, challenge yourself: can you create your forest as an imaginary landscape that can shift and alter as the text dictates and the story develops? I did it with doors and umbrellas floating down from the flies. You could try ropes, or scaffold pipes or even chairs.

I use chairs constantly in the design as well as the rehearsal process. I see an actor sitting in the middle of a space on a chair. A humble bentwood chair. He might be powerful, as with King Lear at the beginning of that play; or vulnerable, as with Lear later in the same scene when his daughter rejects him. He stands up, the chair topples over and chaos ensues. Someone picks up the chair and threatens with it, as a weapon. Edgar entwines himself inside it and we create his hovel as Poor Tom. Simple, poetic, theatrical.

So, start with the actor in space and not with a concept.

In this regard, the experiments in theatre in the round since the Second World War are particularly useful.

'In The Round'

In the twentieth century, directors and actors tried to get to the very *essence* of theatre. Peter Brook argued that all you needed was an actor, an audience and a space; this can be as simple as a carpet thrown on the ground.

By gathering the audience *around* the actors, you are placing the characters, the text and the action quite literally at the centre of the experience. You will find that with most texts, whether it be Shakespeare or Caryl Churchill, you don't need much more. Maybe a bit of furniture.

The **entrances and the axes** of the stage become particularly important in this format. On the few occasions that I have worked 'in the round', I have found that a strong dominant axis and a key 'number 1' entrance have proved invaluable. You can think of your stage as a compass: N S E W.

When I directed Ibsen's *A Doll's House* in the round at Stratford, I created a clear North/South axis (Figure 2). It gave impact and drama to the arrival of Krogstad and Torvald and, as the play progressed, gained more and more significance until Nora's final exit when she leaves her husband and children and slams the door. The entrance was no more than a void, a gap between sections of the auditorium, but it accumulated force and meaning, which I enhanced with lighting. The use of this entrance reflected the very subject of the drama. Under what circumstances should Nora walk out on her husband and children? Her exit became a release from prison and it was her husband who remained locked up.

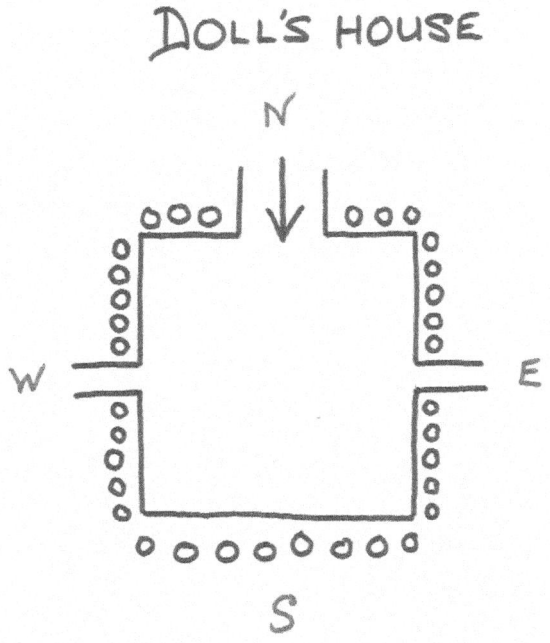

Figure 2 *Doll's house. Drawing courtesy of Adrian Noble.*

As practice, you should take *A Midsummer Night's Dream* and do an 'in the round' exercise. Cut out a circle of paper or cardboard and with other strips of card or even pencils, work out the entrances and the axes of the action. Maybe East/West for Titania/Oberon? Experiment.

Also, in the round, you will discover what you *don't* need. Large items of furniture can easily give you sightline problems and may well obstruct easy movement of the actors around the stage. This is particularly important because actors will have to maintain contact with the whole 360 degrees of the audience. Also, ask yourself: can I use the space above the stage or below it? Can I hang things very simply from the rig, or just the ceiling if you are in a small fringe venue? Is there any space underneath the stage that I can exploit? You might be lucky!

'Thrust' Stages

Another exciting post-Second World War development has been the explosion of new theatres built with thrust stages, with the audience on three sides of the actors.

These spaces have their ancestry in the Elizabethan theatres used by Shakespeare or the inn yards used by theatre companies 'on tour'. The action would take place on the floor of the inn yard or on a simple zip-up stage and the audience would be gathered around, some of them, presumably, looking down from windows or balconies. These thrust stages, also known as courtyard theatres, seem to chime well with our more democratic, less deferential era. They are particularly suitable to productions of Shakespeare's plays, but are surprisingly sympathetic to the plays of Chekov or Pinter, indeed any play that has a poetic dimension.

Here, as in the round, entrances, exits and axes are of great significance. Very often diagonals need to be used if the entrances are downstage left and downstage right. Look at the Swan Theatre, Stratford-upon-Avon (Figure 3).

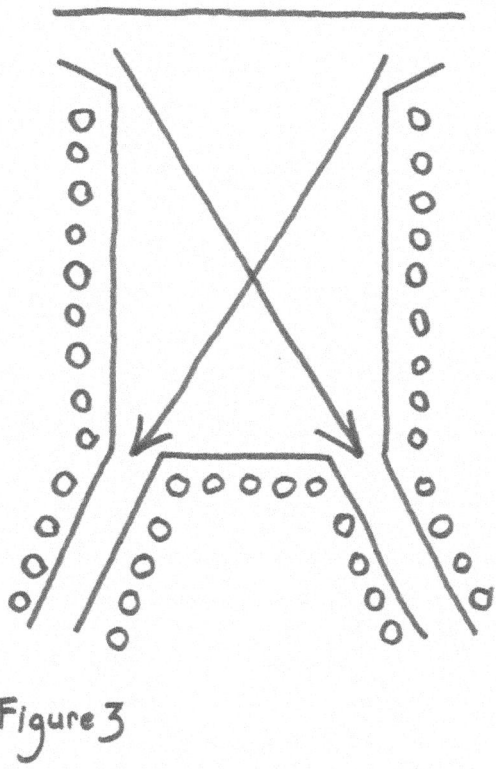

Figure 3 *Swan Theatre, Stratford-upon-Avon. Drawing courtesy of Adrian Noble.*

There is, of course, the upstage wall and the temptation here is to create a 'wall of information'; an all purpose background that is suitable to all moments of the play. I try to avoid this by approaching the space more as a theatre in the round. What are the dynamic entrances? Principal axes? Do I really need anything at the back? As noted, the back walls of theatres are often textured with the very history of the building. Start with nothing, then add a wall or edifice of some kind. Better still, is it possible for this wall to change and adapt with the action? What are my options? Can I create a 'wall' of light using strong downlight and a bit of smoke in the air (known kindly as 'atmos').

As in the round, you must be frugal with the amount of furniture you put on the stage and the height of each piece.

Technology of Design: How to Get from A to B

Once you have explored the space of the play in whatever configuration you are working in, proscenium, thrust, in the round, you and your designer will have to consider the technology of the production, by which I mean **how to get from one scene to another**. In many respects, this will predicate the *style* of your show.

Shakespeare and all the Elizabethan/Jacobean playwrights were writing for a stage that was almost completely empty, except, perhaps, for the odd bench or throne. So there is no time or opportunity built into the script for set changes. The assumption in the text is that one character enters speaking while another actor is still making his/her exit. This creates a rhythm and a forward energy that you are wise to embrace. So beware of elaborate, lengthy scene changes mid-act.

What are your options? How can you make the changes an integral, creative aspect of your production? In a studio theatre you will certainly be limited by budgetary constraints; regard this as a plus – it requires you to be inventive. Think about using furniture that can service more than one scene and perhaps accumulate significance. Prepare a plan for scene changes *at the design stage*, otherwise you could be badly hampered when you finally arrive on the stage. Do you want your actors to move the scenery? In character or not? Do you need stage hands? How many? Do you want the audience to watch the changes, known as 'open' changes? Do you want to choreograph the changes? By which I don't mean dance them, though this is an option, probably not desirable except in musicals! All these decisions affect the *style* of the show.

Try to use this challenge to sharpen your concept of the play. Pay particular attention to the **moments of revelation** in your production, which are often the links between one part of the story and the next. Examples: Lear and the Fool arriving at the heath during the storm, the arrival of the Players in *Hamlet*. You won't necessarily need great scenic resources. But don't be afraid of a few big, bold gestures. The King and Fool could appear over the far horizon of the stage, or walk up the aisle of the theatre. An actor could walk onto the stage and tip over the throne, followed by a powerful elemental crash with sound. The storm breaks!

Identify two or three links or bridges and try to create dramatic moments that will help you shift between one movement of the play to the next. These might well not have a scenic solution, but they are very important; prepare for them.

Colour, Texture and Decoration

These matters are important, but secondary. Colour influences the audience's perception of space. A dark set will usually close the space down; it will make it easier to isolate areas of the action with light, or even focus right down to a single spot for a soliloquy. With a light-coloured set, you may communicate a lighter atmosphere, but light will tend to bounce around. When considering colour, it is best to consult with your lighting designer. A well-lit cyclorama can be hugely helpful to change the mood and to 'glue' scenes together.

Colour and texture will also help communicate the world of the play. *Romeo and Juliet* is urban; interiors, street life, night scenes, real beds, real furniture. The *Dream* is rural; open air, magic, a forest, a fairy bower. So choice of texture will help *lead* the production and help reveal the world of the play. Do you choose wood? Or stone? Or grass? ? Do you watch the action through a scrim? Old floorboards? Whatever your budget, seek out images of colour and texture and pin them on the wall.

EUREKA!

Human creativity obeys no rules of time, sequence or rationale. Sometimes you or your designer will be ambushed. The perfect solution to your design challenge might come at any stage in the process. This may take the form of a single, simple architectural solution. This is where your instinct comes in. Does it *feel* right? Does it *excite* you? Does it tell the story? Does it allow you to fully explore the journey of the play that you have identified. If it does, run with it!

This has happened to me on a few occasions and it is very exciting. Tobias Hoheisel came up with the idea of a rotating metal cylinder for the opera *Serse* in Vienna, inside of which we had a verdant forest; outside was barren. It instantly gave me the dialectical tension I was seeking.

At The Other Place in Stratford, David Ultz came up with the idea of a suspended square stage, covered in paper, with audience on four sides. It was the perfect set for a new play about the painter William Hogarth, and very cheap to create.

In such a circumstance, be rigorous in your working through, but **be supportive and welcoming to the designer**. Their job can be as lonely as yours.

Storyboard

Another technique that I have found useful is to storyboard. This is used extensively in film where there are specialist storyboard artists who are spectacularly talented. The idea is to create a series of images from particular moments in the play. They don't need to be elaborate or beautifully executed; their purpose is to allow your designer's imagination to run freely. This can run in parallel to the white card stage.

Throughout the design process, but particularly in the early stages, have the courage to throw things out. Your designer might be resistant to this, but you are wise to follow your instincts. That floor doesn't feel right; chuck it out. It's too cluttered; chuck it out. How about that colour? Change it. As Jean-Louis Barrault said: 'Cling to nothing!'

Show and Tell

So now you have assembled what you hope is the final model. It will probably be painted and might even have pieces of model furniture. Sooner or later you are going to have to reveal your work to a wider and wider group of people. This is always a scary moment, whether it is to fellow students on your drama course or to the Music Director of the Metropolitan Opera.

Show and tell!

My advice is simple: prepare well and give a decent presentation. Whoever it is, they won't know the play as well as you. Explain how you see the story unfold. Wherever possible, show accompanying imagery and references.

It's important that all these people, especially those who are directly working on the production, *buy into your ideas and are excited by them*. The care you take at each stage of presentation will show the respect you have for each group. And at every stage, more and more people will enter the circle of your production. So take care to involve them. And thank them!

FAQ: Design

What if they don't like what we've done?

Listen carefully and respectfully. An outside eye, someone coming to the project fresh, might well have an insight that you can take onboard. Perhaps your ideas aren't as clear to a third party as you thought they were. However, you may well have to stick to your guns and try to persuade them that you are right. Finally, a production can only have one leader. It's not a democracy and you can't please everyone. But it can be lonely and you might feel vulnerable. Think this through. You may well need a friend.

What if my designer and I get stuck?

This happens to everyone! Remember that designers work principally through imagery and not words. Try a new tack. Go back over your wall of ideas. I sometimes look at the work of artists I admire, especially from different disciplines, like Pina Bausch the choreographer. Try storyboarding. I've also found it useful to go on trips together, to art galleries or the movies. Anywhere you can discuss in imagery rather than words. And understand that designers, like all artists, need space and time. Get off their back. Give them time to work things through. They don't stop working just because you're not in the room!

What if someone asks 'What is your concept?'

They will. This happens frequently in the world of opera. I find it reductive and try to avoid the question. Your production is complex, multifaceted and your first loyalty is to the author, who may, of course, be in the room.

When should I involve the lighting designer in the process?

You will find that lighting and costume designers will want to be involved as early as possible. Embrace this, as they are invariably great collaborators. Costume and set designers will, of course, frequently be the same person. A lighting perspective will be extremely useful to your deliberations about the set and can often solve intractable problems. Explain the background to your production, the journey you want to take the audience on and any ideas you may already have, e.g. the entrance of the lovers in the *Dream* described earlier.

Sometimes you will have a different person doing costumes. I prefer to be a little way down the design road before I involve them. Partly so as not to waste their time or mine.

Working with Costume Designers

Costume is the quickest and most immediate way of communicating all sorts of information to an audience about age, status, period as well as character traits that are particular to him or her (e.g. the 'fiery' Tybalt).

As with set designers, take care to choose the right person and brief them thoroughly. Your background analysis and imagery will be enormously helpful to them, even if you are still en route with the set design. Take extra time to talk through your discoveries on character, status, social groupings and family trees. Your designer will want to know if you have chosen a period to set the play in. Will you set *Henry V* in Medieval times or the First World War or during the Falklands war? All these choices are quite valid, but be logical and be rigorous. What is the military world that the play inhabits and what kind of warfare is described? What are the social and political relationships? As an audience member watching a fight scene, I always feel uncomfortable when I hear a character say 'Draw your sword' when they are carrying guns. I'm not stupid and the actors aren't stupid. Cut the lines or rewrite the text, assuming the play is out of copyright.

Your costume designer will want to work closely with the set designer. Encourage this. You want an integrated whole. You want complementary colour palettes and textures.

Costume and the Actor

I would advise you to think of costume as *clothes*, worn in real situations, so they can be created for this particular character, played by that particular actor. As you progress, imagine how this or that design will work from the actor's point of view. Is it *wearable*? They must own the design or it will look uncomfortable, even out of place. Many great actors say they start building their characters from the feet up. They want to get the right shoes or boots and often ask to rehearse in them. Be prepared for actors to ask for some adjustments to the designs. Listen and try to accommodate if you believe this will not compromise the integrity of the production. Otherwise you must support the designer and stand your ground.

Finally I would say that modern dress does not automatically equate with accessibility and period does not necessarily alienate a contemporary, sophisticated audience. I would encourage you to have a high opinion of your audience; modern audiences are experienced and canny. They have been exposed to an explosion of fashion that has ransacked the past and embraced the exotic. They want to be emotionally involved and not led by the nose.

The Director and the Lighting Designer

You should consider consulting your set designer before you appoint a lighting (LX) designer, but this is only a courtesy. Finally you have to have *your* team on board. There are three stages to the process.

1. Briefing. Before rehearsals, at the model stage, talk through your production scene by scene. Use colourful, vivid,

evocative language. 'A door opens and we see a vision of hell.' 'Like a balmy summer's day.' Your LX designer will interpret. A good LX designer will be able to sculpt and frame the actors and carve the space with light. He/she will certainly ask for 'atmos' to help achieve this; a very light mist that picks up the beam of light from the lanterns. Light in this way becomes a crucial part of the scenery. Communicate any special effects that you hope for. For example, ' I want a narrow carpet of light running diagonally across the stage.' Or 'I'd like heavy side light in this scene.' Low side light can 'lift' the actors, which is why it is frequently used in ballet. Backlight can be very dramatic, but tiring for an audience as it can dazzle out the faces. A gloomy lighting state can make comedy very hard to play. Technological advances in lighting have been phenomenal over the last twenty years; lighting can certainly contribute to the punctuation as well as the general 'feel' of a show. The choices available have grown exponentially with the arrival of moving lights. You can feature changes of focus and colour if you believe it supports your production.

2   After a run through. Your LX designer will have seen the choices you have made and will quiz you on details or forewarn you about possible challenges. (At this stage I will usually ask if the production is 'readable'.)

3   During tech and previews, you should place yourself in the auditorium close to the LX board so that you can communicate swiftly and easily. Be honest about visibility. If you think it's too dark, say so. Always try to give notes as soon as poss so the LX team can get straight to work to improve and amend.

6

Design – The Ear

Music

Over the centuries, Shakespeare has inspired great artists from other media and disciplines: painters, choreographers and, especially, composers. Purcell, Verdi and Britten have created wondrous operatic works based upon his plays. Many more have set his songs to music or been influenced by his dramaturgy. I myself have had the good fortune to work with Guy Wolfenden, Ilona Sekacz, Howard Blake, Shaun Davy, Craig Armstrong, Sa DingDing and many others.

Shakespeare clearly understood musical structure, was highly sensitive to musical cadence and alert to the power of music. In the final act of *The Merchant of Venice*, he wrote:

JESSICA
    I am never merry when I hear sweet music.

LORENZO
    The reason is, your spirits are attentive:
    For do but note a wild and wanton herd,
    Or race of youthful and unhandled colts,
    Fetching mad bounds, bellowing and neighing loud,
    Which is the hot condition of their blood;
    If they but hear perchance a trumpet sound,

Or any air of music touch their ears,
You shall perceive them make a mutual stand,
Their savage eyes turn'd to a modest gaze
By the sweet power of music: therefore the poet
Did feign that Orpheus drew trees, stones and floods;
Since nought so stockish, hard and full of rage,
But music for the time doth change his nature.
The man that hath no music in himself,
Nor is not moved with concord of sweet sounds,
Is fit for treasons, stratagems and spoils;
The motions of his spirit are dull as night
And his affections dark as Erebus:
Let no such man be trusted. Mark the music.

(*The Merchant of Venice* 5.1.69–88)

Here, Shakespeare claims a transformative, almost magical power for music. I can't disagree. It can be highly potent stuff and is best used wisely and discretely, in support of the text and the narrative. But a great cue, in the right place, can transform the experience of the audience and give your actors a great lift.

So how should you set about choosing music for your production?

- If at all possible, work with a **living composer** who will create a new score for your production. I managed this at university and worked with the absurdly talented Colin Sell. Circumstances may not allow an original score, so you will need to draw music from existing works (and pay the necessary copyright fees!).

- My own inclination to create three strong movements stems from a desire to articulate the shape, structure and mood of a piece. Brief your composer on your thinking or choose appropriate tracks.

- There is music *of the play* and music *in the play*. Distinguish between the two. Many of Shakespeare's plays have songs or music cues written *in the play*, Feste's songs in *Twelfth Night* for example; as the director you can also choose music *of the play*, music that serves a number of dramatic purposes. The two will, of course, be intimately related. So Shaun Davy wrote wonderful bucolic songs, almost music hall, for the sheep shearing feast in *The Winter's Tale*. He used one of these simple songs in a quite different mood as the basis for the reawakening of Hermione and in a more uplifting manifestation, for the curtain call.

- Music can help create place and occasion. Remember our work on public and private. Howard Blake's score for my *Henry V* gave me the public military excitement of the invasion. We had the resources of the whole Royal Shakespeare Company band at our disposal, but there are ways of creating pomp and circumstance with limited technical kit. Of equal importance, Howard underpinned the private loneliness of the common soldiers in France, far from home. He took a single line of dialogue of the Boy, 'Would I were in an alehouse in London', and wrote a plaintive air that recurred through the play. I even used it when Pistol hears of the death of his wife Mistress Quickly. I asked Patricia Routledge to sing it in the distance, breaking up the lines, forgetting words. It was profoundly moving.

- Music can help create mood and atmosphere. Above, I quoted from *The Merchant of Venice*. I had no musicians at my disposal for my production in San Diego, but those lines put me in mind of Gustav Mahler, so I only used his works throughout the piece. The deep sadness that underlies

Shylock's story was perfectly captured in passages of Mahler's symphonies.

- Music can help you transform from one movement of the play to another or, at a basic level, help you make a scene change. The most mundane action, carting a table off or placing a throne, can be given a little magic. And the great dramatic shifts in the story, the arrival in the Forest of Arden in *As You Like It* or the reading of the names of the dead in *Henry V*, can be given a fitting majesty and potency.

- Try to suggest an optimum length for a cue. Imagine it in your head and time it. Does the cue pick up the mood of the outgoing scene or introduce the next scene? Is the music complementary to the action or contrapuntal?

- Underscore can have a mighty impact. The ubiquity of film and television means that our ears are quite accustomed to underscore. Shakespeare too understood its potency. The above speech in *Merchant* was written to be underscored. Underscore can be very tempting and can transform a pretty ordinary delivery of a speech into something memorable. But there are dangers. My advice would be to use the device sparingly. Does Henry really need his speech 'What's he that wishes so?' underscored? The music can overpower the speech and obscure the changes and generalize the action. You can experiment in rehearsal.

- Music can help create a whole world for your production. You can choose to have music playing while the audience enters. This will help create a particular mood. It can enliven an audience or quieten and settle them. On occasion I have wanted to create a party-like atmosphere, with *Comedy of Errors* for example and asked the musicians to play front of house as the audience arrived. I took this further at the Roundhouse in London with *Pericles*. I wanted to create the best party ever, except you had to pay! So there was live music pre-show, the actors entertained with song, even some acrobatics. Shaun Davy composed a Celtic-based score which helped transport the audience into the romantic world of the play. An energy was released from the audience that we could harness in the performance.

- Consider harnessing the musical skills of your actors. Many will have fine singing voices and some will have skills with instruments. You might need the help of a music director (MD) to fully exploit this resource. I used the voices of the full company to sing a multipart Russian folk song which introduced Constantin's play in the opening act of Chekov's *Seagull*. In a quite different way, I collaborated with the voice coach Cicely Berry and composer Ilona Sekacz to create the storm in *King Lear* using, principally, the human voice. This idea worked wonderfully; the storm was part manifestation of Lear's inner psychological world and part the external natural world. We called it the 'Voice of the Storm'.
- Make a list of all possible music cues and mark them MQ1, MQ2, etc. Try adding labels – 'We hear the sound of Paradise' or 'Quicken the pulse', etc.

Sound

Involve a **sound designer** early on in the process. He/she will help facilitate much of the above and will be able to create a whole soundscape if that is what you want. Your sound designer will help to conjure the world of the play.

- Is it rural or urban?
- Is a scene day or night?
- Are the sounds we hear *naturalistic*, i.e. the real sounds you might hear in Verona or at Agincourt, birdsong, street noise, etc. or *realistic* to the production, for example the magical sounds of the island suggested in the *Tempest*.
- The sound designer can enhance and amplify the drama. For example he/she can create a multilayered track of sounds of war to play during the battle of Agincourt.
- He/she can punctuate a scene. For example the sound of a heavy door slamming at particular moments in *Measure for Measure*. Or the sound of a distant scream in *Macbeth*. Such effects can be played subliminally or purposefully, intrusively.
- In some circumstances you might have to amplify or enhance the voices of the actors. Certainly in musicals you will need radio mics to achieve any sort of balance with the band. Sometimes in the open air voices can simply get lost. The practice of enhancement is now common in the US and becoming increasingly the norm in larger spaces in the UK. Be aware: 'micing' or enhancement is quite contentious in some quarters, the argument being that it reduces the range of communication of the human voice and discourages the actor from taking responsibility for projecting to the whole house. It is worth noting that the technology of enhancement has developed exponentially over the last couple of decades.
- Make a list of all possible sound cues and mark them SQ1, SQ2, etc. Add a 'tag' or description.

7

Casting the Play

His playing has become so transparent, so imbued with what he is interpreting, that one no longer sees the performer himself – he is simply a window opening upon a great work of art.
-*À LA RECHERCHE DU TEMPS PERDU*, PROUST

The Actor's World

Theatre making is one of the great collaborative art forms. As a director, you are wise to flip the camera constantly, to look at a situation from a different point of view. Now ponder for a moment the actor's world. I'm addressing, first, the professional theatre.

In the professional world, in the UK and US, the vast majority of actors are *freelance agents*, moving from job to job. There are some semi-permanent ensembles, such as the Royal Shakespeare Company, but these are rare. Most actors make their living from a mixed economy of theatre, film, TV and radio, or voiceovers. For a few highly successful actors, this gives them a large degree of artistic freedom. Many actors welcome the excitement of the 'unknown', the unsolicited script arriving at the door, the telephone call from their agent with an offer. But the majority must endure considerable economic vulnerability. *The director is essentially their employer*, even though his/her name might not be on the pay cheque.

So mutual respect is essential.

The majority of actors in the UK undergo some sort of *vocational training*, usually in one of the drama schools, or perhaps took a degree at university, a route common in the US.

At drama school or university they would certainly have studied *Stanislavski*, indeed some institutions label themselves as 'Method' schools. Most actors you encounter for your production will have absorbed the rudiments of the Method. This may be as basic as identifying with the character or aspects of the character; or it may be a fully formed methodology, depending upon which drama school or university they attended.

Be aware of this.

Many students will have had some instruction in working with *Shakespeare*, though this is rarely adequate. The traditional route for an actor to build up experience in the classics – drama school, years in repertory, then the West End or the National Companies – has long since eroded. This means that many actors you will work with in your Shakespeare production will have limited experience.

Again, be aware of this.

You will certainly find throughout the profession a passion for Shakespeare. This is because his work is the most challenging and the most rewarding. Many actors regard their achievements with Shakespeare as the pinnacle and defining aspect of their career.

If you are a student or a non-professional, you will find all of these features in many of your peer group, or the pool of actors you are looking to work with.

Do I Cast the Actor or the Part?

There are some roles, Henry V, King Lear, Othello, Rosalind, that are so demanding that you are unwise to embark on a production without the right actor in place. These roles require a high level of skill, stamina and sheer ability to *entertain*. And you, as the director, need to build a special relationship to embark on this journey together, for it has to be a *collaboration*. You must share your ideas and build trust. The relationship between director and leading actor can be one of the most rewarding in your life. As I said in the opening chapter, always seek out the finest actors; they may be challenging but will certainly be the most rewarding.

And know this: *good actors attract other good actors to a project.*

So, let's say you have your Romeo and Juliet in place and (preferably), you've talked through your ideas with them. What next?

Here's a question: *do I cast the actor or the part*? Put another way, do you try to attract the best group of actors to your show, even though they are not perfect casting for each part? Or do I try to fit each part like a glove? Of course you want both! I prefer to cast a group of actors and tackle the play together. We know that Shakespeare himself, working with a fixed group of actors at the Globe, was sometimes cast in parts he was not obviously suited to. For example, he played Old Adam in *As You Like It*, while in his early thirties.

This approach also gives you freedom to cast more roles with women and to create an ethnically diverse company. As observed, Shakespeare is not a 'naturalistic' writer and this gives you great opportunities for imaginative casting, free from the restrictions of television 'authentic' casting. Challenge yourself on the *gender* of each part. Challenge yourself on the *ethnicity* of each part. Shakespeare's play often use a template of patriarchal hierarchy. We live in a different, changing world and your production can respond to this imaginatively. Having said that, you as the director must work through the implications of, let's say, casting Mercutio as a woman. I repeat, create a logical world.

Compose your company. When putting together a cast for a Shakespeare play or, for that matter, *any* play, it is best to assemble a range of talents and experience. Older, more experienced actors will usually go out of their way to support younger actors. They may offer advice or pass on skills. This baton passing has been going on for five hundred years and I believe is very healthy. Some directors, however, feel threatened by this, or wish to be the only voice of authority in the room.

What is certain is that when you arrive on Day One of rehearsals, you will have some artists who, without question, will need more help, direction, instruction, than others. Be alert. Be prepared.

Here's an important question: *can all good actors play Shakespeare?* You see an actor being quite marvellous in a police drama on TV. Would he/she be quite marvellous in a Shakespeare play? Or a young actor does a terrific audition with a modern piece or monologue or, as sometimes happens, an improvisation that is totally real and engaging. Can you cast him/her in a leading part? Are the skills easily transferable?

Well, you'd have to explore further. The actor in question clearly has great ability to create an authentic, realistic character; perfect for TV or film. Shakespeare requires an additional skill set, let us call it a parallel skill set, to bring that empathy, that connection to a character who expresses him/herself *entirely* in blank verse. Or at least, heightened language.

Some actors can do both at the very highest level. These are the great artists.

This is the Shakespeare/Method tension; the inside out/outside in tension; the hear a play/see a play tension. We will see in rehearsal that this is one of the most exciting, creative issues you will encounter. But if an actor really can't deal with the language, you're in trouble, because they will come across as weak or from another planet.

The Audition Process

Actors *hate* auditioning. Every actor in the world will have horror stories to tell. These usually involve lack of respect, waste of time, humiliation and discourtesy. Directors are rude, look at their iPhones during the audition, run late and don't apologize, they chat away to their casting director as if the actor didn't exist, they laugh at private jokes. A litany of misery!

Each of these tales is underpinned by the fact that the actor is a supplicant.

As a consequence, actors will avoid auditions as soon as they gain sufficient status. They will meet you 'without prejudice', which means they are sussing *you* out as well. They might meet and read.

Old-fashioned auditions, where an actor comes into the room and performs two monologues, a Shakespeare and a 'modern', with or without introductory chats, have become increasingly rare in 'straight' theatre, or 'legit' as it's called in the States. In musical theatre it is quite usual for a performer of considerable talent and status to come in and sing. It's businesslike and dignified.

It needs to be made clear to the actor *before* the audition what is expected. You will certainly want to find out more about the actor, so leave time for a conversation. Whether this is before or after the audition is up to you. Some actors prefer to come in, do their stuff and then talk; they can thus maintain their focus. Some prefer an 'ice-breaking' chat first.

So,

DO thank them for coming in.

DO try to give immediate, clear, positive feedback on what they have done.

DO study their CV *before* they come in and don't read while they are performing.

DO have water available and throwaway cups.

DO try to get a proper conversation going. How did they think their reading/monologue went? What's their take on the play?

DO try to find a decent-sized room.

DO offer them the opportunity to try again if they wish and you have the time. You can judge how they take direction.

DO consider them for a different part if they are not right for this one.

DO conduct the audition in a friendly but businesslike manner. At this stage they are looking for a job not a friend.

DO make time for **recalls**, on another day, and make it clear to the actor or their representative what you are looking to explore. You may want *x* and *y* actors to read together if the 'chemistry' is important. Let them know this is your intention in advance.

With young or relatively inexperienced actors, it is quite reasonable to ask them to prepare a monologue. It will give you the chance to do some work with them and may well open up your eyes to the range of skills that the actor has and possibly lead to an offer of a different part or a better part.

In some circumstances, you may have the help of a **casting director**. This can be invaluable. They will have an encyclopaedic knowledge of actors and how they did in different roles. They will *know* many more actors than you. So brief them well, let them into your world and they will be great enablers of your vision.

Putting It Together

Try to identify a core group of actors who will sit at the centre of your production and help give it its identity. You may know some or all of this group before auditions.

Get headshots of these and of contenders for all the parts. Put the photo of the leading actor or group on the floor and begin to compose a **company**. Add in photos of other actors you would like to include. By now you will have a good idea of the quality and tone of the production you are planning. Do you need more weight and experience? More women? A more diverse cast? Are you *excited* by the cast that is emerging?

Not all the offers you make will be accepted, for a variety of reasons. Don't be disheartened. Rethink. Try another actor. Slowly (usually!), your company will emerge.

Before we head down the road to rehearsal, let's take another Awayday. Let's explore in more detail how an actor *works*, what method he/she uses. Let's meet Konstantin Stanislavski.

8
Awayday 2: Stanislavski and Actioning

Konstantin Stanislavski (1863–1938) was a highly influential Russian actor, director and teacher. His analysis and practice have impacted generations of theatre makers and it is important that all directors appreciate the tenets of his work. Most drama schools run their acting courses on Stanislavskian lines and most actors will have absorbed the principles of the 'Method', wherever they trained. This chapter will give you an insight into how your actors will approach and develop their roles and useful analytical tools for scene work.

A key word in the understanding of Stanislavski is 'identification'. The actor identifies with the character and shifts his/her centre towards that of the character he/she is playing. The essence of the character overlaps and consumes that of the actor. I remember waiting for my interview for admission at Drama Centre, London. The final-year students, earning a few quid at weekends for shepherding hopeful auditionees, would whisper: 'If they ask you why you want to become an actor, whatever you say, don't say it's to express yourself. Tell them it's about *transformation*.' That was pretty good advice. In many ways, the job of the actor is transform him/herself into another human being.

Think about yourself. In many ways we improvise every moment of our lives. We make choices, we make decisions, we negotiate, *we take actions*. Sometimes these are simple everyday actions: I choose to go for a walk in the park or choose this particular brand of breakfast cereal. Sometimes they are more profound: I choose to pursue this career or this particular lifestyle. Most daily actions will be made unconsciously, but they will be governed by your tastes, your situation, your values, your education, your hopes and ambitions in life. In other words by your character.

How did Stanislavski analyse this? He said that human beings (characters) have actions, objectives and super objectives. Example: my *action* is to make my co-workers respect me, in order to achieve my *objective*, which is to have a successful career, in order to achieve my *super objective*, which is a life of wealth and happiness. In other words, we are driven by *wants*, whether conscious or unconscious, a useful concept for actors to use. A common mistake of many actors is that their wants are insufficiently strong, their super objectives need tuning and sharpening. We have noticed already that many of Shakespeare's characters are driven and often have quite extreme emotions. Remember Rosalind in *As You Like It* talking about love to Celia; 'Love is merely a madness'. Later in that scene she says 'I cannot be out of the sight of Orlando. I'll go find a shadow and sigh till he come.' This emotional drive makes them dramatic and exciting to watch. So, what does King Lear *want* when he divides the kingdom? Your answer will form the basis of your interpretation of the play. When I directed *Lear* in Stratford in 1993, Robert Stephens played him as a very selfish, short-sighted, wilful man, locked in his own vanity. He was violent and tetchy. He wanted to keep power and indulge himself in old age. The events of the play taught him wisdom and he found peace. His super objective changed during the course of the play. Michael Gambon, who I directed much earlier, made Lear more political, more scheming, much more reliant on the input of the Fool to make sense of the world; he wanted wisdom and harmony. He got neither and we made the final movement of the play bleak and unforgiving. Two quite different, contrasting interpretations.

Let's go back to **actions**. When analysing actions, I find it useful to describe them in *transitive* terms. In other words, one character is trying to change another. Sometimes it helps to add the word 'make' in a sentence. So I make you listen or I make you aware of another way of thinking or, simply, I make you laugh. Look at this speech from *Henry V*. His men are at a low ebb and fear defeat at the hands of the more numerous and much better armed French.

WESTMORELAND

    O that we now had here
    But one ten thousand of those men in England
    That do no work to-day!

KING HENRY V

                What's he that wishes so?
My cousin Westmoreland? No, my fair cousin:
If we are mark'd to die, we are enow   20
To do our country loss; and if to live,
The fewer men, the greater share of honour.
God's will! I pray thee, wish not one man more.
By Jove, I am not covetous for gold,
Nor care I who doth feed upon my cost;
It yearns me not if men my garments wear;

Such outward things dwell not in my desires:
But if it be a sin to covet honour,
I am the most offending soul alive.
No, faith, my coz, wish not a man from England:
God's peace! I would not lose so great an honour
As one man more, methinks, would share from me
For the best hope I have. O, do not wish one more!
Rather proclaim it, Westmoreland, through my host,
That he which hath no stomach to this fight,
Let him depart; his passport shall be made
And crowns for convoy put into his purse:
We would not die in that man's company
That fears his fellowship to die with us.
This day is called the feast of Crispian:
He that outlives this day, and comes safe home,
Will stand a tip-toe when the day is named,
And rouse him at the name of Crispian.
He that shall live this day, and see old age,
Will yearly on the vigil feast his neighbours,
And say 'To-morrow is Saint Crispian:'
Then will he strip his sleeve and show his scars.
And say 'These wounds I had on Crispin's day.'
Old men forget: yet all shall be forgot,
But he'll remember with advantages
What feats he did that day: then shall our names.
Familiar in his mouth as household words
Harry the king, Bedford and Exeter,
Warwick and Talbot, Salisbury and Gloucester,
Be in their flowing cups freshly remember'd.
This story shall the good man teach his son;
And Crispin Crispian shall ne'er go by,

> From this day to the ending of the world,
> But we in it shall be remember'd;
> We few, we happy few, we band of brothers;   60
> For he to-day that sheds his blood with me
> Shall be my brother; be he ne'er so vile,
> This day shall gentle his condition:
> And gentlemen in England now a-bed
> Shall think themselves accursed they were not here,
> And hold their manhoods cheap whiles any speaks
> That fought with us upon Saint Crispin's day.
>
> (*King Henry V* 4.3.16–67)

Henry is faced with a massive problem here. All the principal military leaders are there, listening to Westmoreland whose words can only undermine confidence. So ask yourself, what does Henry *do*? Not what does he *say*, what does he *do*? What is his **action**? Presumably, he wants to transform the situation and make them fight. That is the action. Now, how does he do that? What *activities* does he use to achieve this action? Perhaps he makes them believe in themselves, or perhaps he makes them feel ashamed of themselves or perhaps he makes them feel aggressive, perhaps he makes them feel special, like heroes. When my Henry, Ken Branagh, started working on this speech, he positively *threw* energy at it, like paint on a wall. Quite soon he focused it right down and found many variations and subtleties. By the time we opened, his soldiers would have followed him to the moon. You can go through the speech and mark up different activities. The moment that you break down a long speech like this into constituent activities, you guard against generalization; you can use this analysis to help your actors be specific. The action is achieved through transitive activities. These are his means to an end and are all active and dynamic. The objective is to win the battle. The super objective is to win the war or ensure a lasting peace or legitimize his claim to the throne, depending on your interpretation.

So, to sum up:

ACTIVITY <<ACTION <<OBJECTIVE <<SUPER OBJECTIVE

In our daily lives, we rarely articulate these actions and objectives, but they drive our behaviour none the less and they frame our personality. In rehearsal, however, actions and objectives are essential to create a dynamic, exciting, focused production. But beware of piling in the first few times your actor tries the speech; give him or her space and time to explore. But in your prep, get a clear idea of actions and objectives.

Now consider **the marriage of actions with the tools Shakespeare offers** to the actor. We explored these tools in Chapter 4, 'Awayday 1: Dramatic Energy (How Does He Do It?)'. Let's have a look at Henry's speech. We know his action, let's suggest activities that further the action. You might find it helpful to have a thesaurus to hand to identify just the right specific word.

First of all, look at the **structure**. I said in the earlier chapter that every speech has a beginning, a middle and an end. So, try to divide this speech into three. The first movement is just four lines long, taking us up to 'The fewer men, the greater share of honour', where Henry sets out his position. This is the newspaper headline. Brief, uncompromising, direct, ending with the word 'honour'. He makes them revalue their situation. The second section takes us through to line 39.

> We would not die in that man's company
> That fears his fellowship to die with us.

The word 'honour' is used twice in this section and Henry uses it to set out his values in contrast to the man who 'fears his fellowship'. Of course this is highly manipulative, but the stakes are literally life or death. This section is inspirational but he also surprises and perhaps shocks them by offering a ticket home. The third section, which takes us through to the end, is fascinating; he *mythologizes* the soldiers who stay to fight. He makes them special.

There are no **metaphors** in this speech; it is hard and direct. But he quite literally creates a myth, there on the spot. It is inspired. It is the creation of this myth in the third section that allows him to fulfil the action. As with all metaphors, I suggest that this comes out of the character's unconscious. It is invented in the moment as Henry clocks what day this is. And as a Catholic, he would have been finely tuned to the calendar of feast days. Thus Henry makes his soldiers see themselves not as victims but as heroes. Winston Churchill used exactly the same rhetorical device in his speeches during the Second World War, especially following the evacuation at Dunkirk and after the Battle of Britain. Look them up.

The situation is dangerous and there is a clock ticking. Henry uses **apposition** right through this speech to achieve his action. It is direct and uncompromising. There is an overarching apposition between those who leave and return to England and those who stay and fight. In the first movement the headline is made clear through apposition:

> If we are mark'd to die, we are enow
> To do our country loss; and if to live,
> The fewer men, the greater share of honour.

Die/live … … fewer/greater

It's urgent and direct; he *makes* them face up to the reality of the situation and he *makes* them see a glimpse of something precious ... honour. Go through the speech with a highlighter and mark up where Shakespeare uses apposition.

Consider his use of **metre and pulse**. Much of the speech is quite regular which gives it a strong forward momentum, appropriate to the situation and the action. Look for where he goes off rhythm. On line 23, the beginning of section 2, he gives you two strong beats to kick off the line:

> God's will! I pray thee, wish not one man more

Bang! Bang! He alerts or he pounces or he ambushes. He repeats the trick a few lines later:

> God's peace! I would not lose so great an honour

And again:

> Old men forget: yet all shall be forgot

Old men, strong, strong and then he uses a memorable juxtaposition.

Line endings always point to the urgency of the action. Henry's first words, 'What's he that wishes so?' finishes the half line of Westmoreland's. So Henry has to grab the moment before his cousin's doubts spread through the camp into mutiny. He alerts, he ambushes. Don't let the actor pause before the word 'What's'. Straight in. He'll probably need to be listening somewhere onstage. Again, no pause after the word 'Westmoreland'. Drive on to the line ending. Henry must *make them listen* and take control. Look for other examples in the speech where he has a full stop or semicolon in the middle of a line. Never pause at this point, always drive on to the line ending because the action requires quick nimble thinking. This is a rhetorical device used constantly in debates, the Houses of Parliament or Congress. It keeps control with the speaker. And keep an eye on the choice of words at the end of the line. The word 'honour' sits at the end of the line three times and 'Crispian' four times. He's a good politician; he controls the message!

Also, check out Henry's use of **vocabulary**. In many ways this is a straightforward direct speech, but Shakespeare gives you clues as to the weight of certain ideas. In particular look for monosyllabic lines, for example lines 61–62:

> For he to-day that sheds his blood with me
> Shall be my brother.

With those words, Henry amazes his soldiers; it's an extraordinary offer from a Medieval monarch. And he amazes them by use of monosyllables. When you see a monosyllabic line, or part of a line that is monosyllabic, try slowing up. It will make the line 'land' more. And with the above, play the line through to the end, 'me', and give a slight beat before answering 'Shall be my brother'. In rehearsal I sometimes make parts of a speech into a dialogue to improve the shape and spring of the verse. So here, after the actor says 'with me', I will say 'yes, what happens to him?' And the actor answers 'Shall be my brother'. It may sound daft, but it's highly effective. And it reinforces the Stanislavskian activity, to make the soldiers feel special, even privileged.

Ok. Back to final preparations for rehearsals which are getting closer. Back to the text and consider whether or not you want to direct a full version or you want to cut.

9

To Cut or Not to Cut, That is the Question

When I was running the RSC, one of the most common complaints from actors about their directors was the late arrival of cuts to the text. Directors would present quite significant cuts late on in rehearsal, sometimes during previews. From the director's point of view, this is quite understandable and I have to put my hand up and confess that I've done this more times than I care to remember. When you start running the play or sections of the play, it can become evident that the shape of the play is not evolving as you hoped, or such and such subplot is outstaying its welcome or perhaps it's just too darned long!

Before we tackle the whys and hows of cutting, consider for a moment **the actor's and writer's viewpoints**. An **actor** doesn't just say the lines in the right order; he/she will have created a series of interconnected thoughts and emotions that deliver the text, the context, the rhythm and the weight of the lines. If you hack out twenty lines at a particular moment, he/she will have to re-weave the thread and re-assemble the tapestry. This is quite doable and all professional actors are used to this exercise. But there is much work to be done and practice time must be provided.

When Shakespeare's plays were premiered, the **author** was, of course, present and might well have been playing a small part. We know rehearsal time was short. We can assume that Shakespeare was both practical and pragmatic and can imagine a constant, speedy dialogue between stage and auditorium about cuts and rewrites. We can even imagine disagreements between William and Richard Burbage who, as leading actor, was the de facto director.

Nowadays, in exactly the same way, playwrights are either in rehearsal or constantly available for the first production of their plays. I had no desire to cut a single line from Brian Friel's *The Home Place* when I directed the premiere in Dublin. I thought it was perfect. There was disagreement with the producer of the West End transfer about whether to have an intermission. Brian stuck to his guns, the interval stayed and he went on to win the *Evening Standard* award for best new play. I had no desire to cut any of Tom Stoppard's lines from *Travesties* at the Barbican. Indeed he helpfully offered to write me a few extra lines to cover a particularly tricky scene change. What a gent! John Dexter and Arnold Wesker, two very great artists, famously disagreed, with John shouting into the darkened stalls at the Royal Court: 'Arnold, if you don't shut up, I'll direct this play as you wrote it.'

So, if you're lucky enough to get the opportunity to direct a new play, whether it be from a student or an established playwright, give proper respect, collaborate don't dictate. Listen and be courteous. And be aware that some writers will not countenance cuts or alterations to the text after the first production. The estate of Samuel Beckett, Harold Pinter or Brian Friel will not take kindly to you hacking about the text.

Shakespeare, of course, is dead and out of copyright, but, I believe, should still be treated with respect. As should your actors. So, approach cutting the play with respect and rigour. Try to arrive in the rehearsal room with a script cut in advance; give the cuts to your actors as early as possible, even before rehearsals begin, then be alert to any alterations you need to make as the work progresses.

Let's consider why you might cut and how you might do it.

Length

There are several issues here. Our modern sensibility is tuned to short, sharp, episodic experience. Our innate hunger for narrative is prompted and prodded by contemporary film and TV into a near frenzy. You don't have to play to this, but you need to be aware of it. It is, of course, possible for theatre to offer a welcome antidote. The unspoken, unsigned contract that exists between audience and actor when he/she walks out onstage is unique and you have the potential to offer something quite special, out of the ordinary. Our day-long, nine-hour cycle of Shakespeare's early history plays which I entitled *The Plantagenets*, sold like hot cakes. There was a tangible yearning for the long, epic, cathartic experience.

In my view, it is quite acceptable to cut a play to achieve the length you believe is right for your particular circumstances. You may decide that for an outdoor student production a running time of two hours is appropriate. Firstly, **work out how many lines you need to cut** to achieve this. Look up how many lines in the complete text. Now, read aloud two or three sections of one hundred lines each, taken from different parts of the play and time them on your watch or phone. Now do the maths. Divide the number of lines you have read by the time it took. You will find that Shakespeare's plays read at between seventeen and twenty-two lines per minute. Divide the total number of lines in the play by the 'lines per minute' figure and you can tell how long an uncut version of the play would read. Now calculate how many lines need to go to achieve your two-hour ideal time, taking into account intermission time (assuming you take one) and a bit of extra time for scene changes, gales of laughter (if appropriate) and countless rounds of applause.

Now set about cutting the text. You should decide or simply *sense* what kind of experience you want to create and cut accordingly. This can either be an exercise in butchery or it can be a creative act that helps to shape the play and achieve your vision.

Shape

One practical way to assess where to cut, or indeed whether to cut or edit a play, is to create a **time line**. Shakespeare was the master at condensing or eliding time, which has the effect of heightening the tension and quickening the drama.

Take *Macbeth* for example. If you write down the time line, you will discover that just a few hours pass between the witches' prophecy that opens the play and the assassination of Duncan the king, and just a few hours more until Banquo is murdered and his ghost appears at the feast. The plotting is deliberately fast, there is not a second to draw breath, no time for anyone to question what is really happening. Shakespeare doesn't even show us the moment that Macbeth seizes the throne. It happens between scenes.

So make a list, write down the exact time and day of each scene. You will find that the above action takes place over little more than thirty hours and most of the action takes place at night. This time line will immediately give you ideas about staging the play and, certainly, about lighting the play. It may give you ideas about the political setting of the play. He's describing a coup d'etat that happens very, very fast. There are, sadly, many contemporary equivalents. When I directed Verdi's opera version in New York, I set the story during the breakup of the former Yugoslavia in the 1990s. It worked perfectly and I discovered that Verdi had retained the terrific forward movement that Shakespeare creates.

So you may well not want to cut much of this opening movement or if you do, use your cuts to sharpen even further the headlong motion of the drama. Now pursue your time line to the end of the play. You will find that time passes between scenes, weeks, possibly months; and then in the last act, there is an elision of time and the action can be measured in minutes rather than hours. You as the director must make the choices: perhaps it is wise to allow a relaxation of tension in the middle around the 'England' scene? Or perhaps you want to keep up a keen pace by cutting into that scene. You should certainly consider tightening the action in the last twenty minutes by some judicious pruning. You will find that pace and cuts to the text are intertwined. Macbeth is, essentially, a political thriller and your cuts can sharpen the focus.

The time line of *The Winter's Tale* is brilliant and bold. The play falls into three clear movements: Sicily, Bohemia and Sicily again. If you create a precise time line of the first Sicilian section, you will find only a matter of hours pass between Leontes' first outbreak of jealousy in Act 1 and his wife Hermione's apparent death during her show trial with a huge amount of action taking place in the meantime, not least the birth of a baby girl to the Queen. This condensation of action, this elision of time, gives you a clue how to direct the opening acts. Shakespeare wants this tight, almost melodramatic. The pace of your production, the tightening of the 'edit' between scene and scene will reinforce the drama and will tell a lot about the precipitous, obsessive nature of sexual jealousy. So as the director, you may want to tighten the screws even further by cuts. For example, in Act 2 Scene 1, Leontes confronts his wife and a violent exchange takes place. In my production, he struck his wife across the face, properly rehearsed with a fight director, and she fell to the floor. I tightened the dialogue prior to this event to make it more sudden and unexpected, and then cut into the following scene between the King and Antigonus after Hermione has been sent to prison. So when Paulina visits Hermione in Act 2 Scene 2 and discovers she has given birth, the audience immediately connected the premature arrival of the baby with the domestic violence we have witnessed.

Let's look at the detail of how this works. In this passage, Leontes clears his son from the room and confronts his wife. I have marked the cuts I used.

LEONTES
Bear the boy hence. He shall not come about her.
Away with him, and let her sport herself
With that she's big with, for 'tis Polixenes
Has made thee swell thus.

(A Lady exits with Mamillius.)

HERMIONE
But I'd say he had not,
~~And I'll be sworn you would believe my saying,~~
~~Howe'er you lean to th' nayward.~~

LEONTES
~~You, my lords,~~
Look on her, mark her well. ~~Be but about~~
~~To say 'She is a goodly lady,' and~~
~~The justice of your hearts will thereto add~~
~~'Tis pity she's not honest, honorable.'~~
~~Praise her but for this her without-door form,~~
~~Which on my faith deserves high speech, and straight~~
~~The shrug, the 'hum,' or 'ha,' these petty brands~~
~~That calumny doth use—O, I am out,~~
~~That mercy does, for calumny will sear~~
~~Virtue itself—these shrugs, these 'hum's and 'ha's,~~
~~When you have said she's goodly, come between~~
~~Ere you can say she's honest. But~~ And be 't known, 76
From him that has most cause to grieve it should be,
She's an adult'ress.

HERMIONE
Should a villain say so,
The most replenished villain in the world,
He were as much more villain. You, my lord,
Do but mistake.

LEONTES
You have mistook, my lady,
Polixenes for Leontes. ~~O thou thing,~~
~~Which I'll not call a creature of thy place~~
~~Lest barbarism, making me the precedent,~~
~~Should a like language use to all degrees,~~
~~And mannerly distinguishment leave out~~
~~Betwixt the prince and beggar.~~ I have said
She's an adult'ress; I have said with whom.

> More, she's a traitor, and Camillo is
> A federary with her, ~~and one that knows~~
> ~~What she should shame to know herself~~
> ~~But with her most vile principal: that she's~~
> ~~A bed-swerver, even as bad as those~~
> ~~That vulgars give bold'st titles;~~ ay, and privy
> To this their late escape.
>
> HERMIONE
> No, by my life,
> Privy to none of this.
>
> <div align="right">(<i>The Winter's Tale</i> 2.1.59–96)</div>

I kept the argument direct and forceful and therefore violent. Where possible, I preserved the metre. For example, in Leontes' last speech above, 'ay, and privy' flows directly from 'federary with her' both in scansion, but crucially in argument. Test your cuts out loud; is the argument clear, is it logical? You might have to make minor adjustments. For example on line 76, I changed the word 'but' to 'and' which flows better.

Shakespeare plays more time games in this act. We learn that Polixenes has fled the country in 'real' time following Leontes' first jealousy, but, minutes after Leontes learns of this, we hear that he has sent to Delphi for a judgement on his wife. The envoy returns hours later, apparently after twenty-three days and Leontes orders the trial of his wife for treason. This elision of time only adds to the drama and rarely disturbs an audience.

The hurtling character of the Sicilian Act gives way to the freer, bucolic, pastoral scenes in Bohemia. The character of Time him/herself appears, to fast forward the action. You can choose a quite different pace here, with time and space for song and dance. The return to Sicily is imbued with a sense of loss and consequently the pace is more legato. I didn't want to rush these scenes and so I put in cuts to ease the time pressure.

There are times when you want the play to simply get a move on. Instead of rushing lines, slim the scene right down. Here's Paris arriving at Juliet's tomb with his Page. We know that Friar Lawrence's plan has failed and that Romeo is on his way back from Mantua in a desperate state.

> PARIS
> Give me thy torch, boy. Hence and stand aloof.
> ~~Yet put it out, for I would not be seen.~~
> Under yond yew trees lay thee all along,
> ~~Holding thy ear close to the hollow ground.~~
> So shall no foot upon the churchyard tread
> ~~(Being loose, unfirm, with digging up of graves)~~
> But thou shalt hear it. Whistle then to me
> ~~As signal that thou hearest something approach.~~
> Give me those flowers. Do as I bid thee. Go.
> (*Romeo and Juliet* 5.3.1–9)

The scene is lightened by 50 per cent and the forward motion is maintained.

A few more thoughts to consider when cutting. As well as preserving the flow of thought and speech and, where possible, the metre, pay attention to metaphors and conceits, which can extend over several lines. Here's part of the dialogue between Mercutio and Benvolio, taunting Romeo who is listening behind a wall:

> MERCUTIO
> I conjure thee by Rosaline's bright eyes,
> By her high forehead, and her scarlet lip,
> By her fine foot, straight leg, and quivering thigh,

>   And the demesnes that there adjacent lie,
>   That in thy likeness thou appear to us.
>
> BENVOLIO
>   An if he hear thee, thou wilt anger him.
>
> MERCUTIO
>   This cannot anger him. ~~'Twould anger him~~
>   ~~To raise a spirit in his mistress' circle~~
>   ~~Of some strange nature, letting it there stand~~
>   ~~Till she had laid it and conjured it down.~~
>   ~~That were some spite.~~ My invocation
>   Is fair and honest. In his mistress' name,
>   I conjure only but to raise up him.
>
>   (*Romeo and Juliet* 2.1.17–29)

This cut preserves the metre, preserves the thought and maintains the metaphor, the 'game' of conjuring.

Be aware that some actors in your production might have only ten lines in the whole show; if you cut five of them, you have cut 50 per cent of their part. Be sensitive.

Oh, and beware of laugh lines. Don't cut a 'punch line' nor the necessary build up to a laugh. I knew a director who had the unerring talent to kill the laughs.

Choice of Edition

Finally consider **choice of edition**.

There are now many first-rate editions of Shakespeare's texts on the market. You will want one that has a good, easy-to-read font, especially as your actors will be carrying their books around with them for a while. Choose one that has some smart explanatory notes but avoid those that have the notes underneath on the same page as the text. This inevitably means that there are far fewer lines of text per page, making it harder to see the overall shape of a speech or scene. Especially if you have introduced some cuts. I would also recommend having two or three other editions available in the rehearsal room for reference. For this book, I have used the Arden Third Series for my references, which is excellent.

10

The Rehearsal Plan

Rehearsals are getting closer. You've done your analysis, you've prepared the text, you've agreed a design, you've cast the play. Now try to *conceptualize* the rehearsals. Try to *imagine* a rough shape. **Rehearsals have a beginning, a middle and a nearly-at-the-end.** Start drawing together the knowledge you have built up in your preparatory work and in the preceding chapters.

You need a **clear road map**. Then if you want to make a detour to explore this or that or need to divert around an unexpected obstacle or problem, you have the plan to reach your destination. I'd advise that you sketch out your plan on paper. The best rehearsal process will always contain a considerable degree of improvisation on behalf of the director. By which I mean thinking on your feet. This is best done when you have a strong plan in your back pocket!

I'm going to pretend that you have a three-week rehearsal period. You may have more or less; it may be strung out over many weeks mainly in the evenings if you are a student; for the purpose of this exercise, it doesn't matter. We will explore the narrative of rehearsals, the journey of rehearsals with a beginning, a middle and a never-quite-at-the-end.

Most of the following pertains *whatever* play you are rehearsing.

Remember this:

You are not alone.

No two directors will agree on the best way to conduct rehearsals. Most directors will adapt their methods according to the circumstances. The demands of a Shakespeare play are different from a modern classic or a new play. You may have a highly experienced cast or a very young cast. There may be twenty actors in the room or three. A few directors have developed a method of rehearsing that never changes from play to play. I want you to develop your own methodology that you can adapt and tailor to different circumstances. This chapter will help you.

You are not alone. Here's how some of your predecessors have done it:

The Traditional Way of Organizing Rehearsals

1. Introduce the cast, show the model and give guidance as to the kind of production you are aiming for. Show the costume designs.
2. Read the play.
3. Start 'blocking' the play, chronologically. Blocking means the moves the actors make during the course of a scene. (Numbers 1 to 3 will take place on the first day.)
4. Block the entire play.
5. Commence run throughs, interspersed with notes and any reworking necessary.

6. Final run through, open to other interested parties (lighting, sound, dressers, management, etc.).
7. Technical rehearsal and opening.

This method developed in weekly 'rep' when you only had a single working week to prepare a production, while the actors were performing another play in the evening. It is an efficient way of delivering a product, but there is no time for debate or exploration and little time for originality. In those days, it was the *only* way to work and the productions often gave enormous pleasure to audiences. Thankfully, the days of weekly rep have passed, but the straightjacket methodology still persists and, with it, the deadly hand of cliché.

If you have a three-week rehearsal, or the equivalent over a longer period, it is quite possible to work in a creative, organic fashion and produce an original production.

Basic Aims of Rehearsal

- To enable the cast to enter the world of the play
- To enable the cast to enter the world of your rehearsal
- To enable the cast to work to their very highest potential
- To enable a cast of individuals to become a company
- To tell the story of the play as you have conceived it as clearly and vividly as possible
- To ensure that the necessary skills are worked on, whether these are verse speaking, fights, dances, etc.
- To create an atmosphere and a work ethic in which all the above can be achieved

A rehearsal room is not a democracy and all voices are not equal. You are the leader but there might be actors of great experience and wisdom in the room and you would be foolish to ignore them. You will also find that good ideas can come from the most unexpected corner. A strong, confident director will have the humility and the character to accept the best ideas from whatever source and run with them.

To this end, you should embrace flexibility and be prepared to adjust your thinking on a particular scene or moment. You'll certainly make mistakes. Everybody does. Call a coffee break. Come back and keep moving forward and the process will right itself.

Making a Plan

Question: if the whole rehearsal period is 100 per cent, how might you divide up the time between beginning, middle and nearly-at-the-end? One-third, one-third, one-third? One week, one week, one week? How do you balance the overall period?

Beginning

This might take one day, two or possibly a whole week, depending on the complexity of the play, your relationship with the actors and what you want to achieve. If you know the actors well, you can work more confidently and quickly. But if the text is complex and the world you are seeking to create is subtle and particular, then you might need more time. Let's look at the aims of rehearsal, taking *A Midsummer Night's Dream* as an example.

You want to *enable the cast to enter the world of the play.*

There are at least two worlds, the mortals and the immortals and possibly a subsection for the Mechanicals. So you might consider some group work that will allow you to explore these worlds. I am talking about work *on your feet*. Much can be achieved by looking at books and talking, but exercises, improvisations and movement will work viscerally, and can imprint on the actor's imagination. Additionally, such work can help your cast *enter the world of your rehearsal*. I have always been reluctant to spend too long sitting round and much prefer alternating table work with work on our feet in the space. Make a list of possible exercises and improvisations that will help your cast *imaginatively enter the play and, very importantly, release them physically*. You may not need all, or indeed any, of these exercises, but have them in your back pocket, ready. We take an Awayday and go into detail about these exercises when the book takes us inside the rehearsal room.

> You will want to work on the hierarchical nature of the society, mortal and immortal.
> You will want to work on the obsessive nature of love within the play.
> You will want to work on the three movements you have identified, especially the middle movement, chaos, lost in a forest.

We'll find some examples of excercises to help here as well.
Plan to introduce your ideas, your analysis, the structure of the play as you see it. Prepare any visual aid you need, books, paintings, PowerPoint. Prepare to show the set model and costumes.

How do you start to tell the story of the play *as you have conceived it* as clearly and vividly as possible? Do you want a read through? I usually do as it reassures the actors. You can have a read through in the middle of rehearsals if you think it best.

Of great importance is to develop a strategy about the **language** of the play. How do you want your production to *sound*? How do you want the actors to approach the verse? You will have actors of different experience and talents; some quite familiar with Shakespeare's language, some not. I would advise against a 'free for all', in which the loudest voice will prevail. In pre-rehearsal, create a plan of action. Plan to introduce your thinking on verse speaking early on in the process. Language is integral to character. Character should develop in tandem with work on the language. As rehearsals progress, character should be driven by language. With Shakespeare you need to *make* the audience listen. You might opt for formal 'verse classes', but I prefer a more integrated approach. Talk about 'How he does it' at every stage of rehearsal.

Middle

This section of rehearsal is invariably the longest and it is the time when you tell the story of the play and build the necessary skills to achieve this.

During the middle section you want **to stage the whole play**. At my drama school, Drama Centre, London, the word 'blocking' was banned as it suggested a rigid straightjacketed process. The word 'placing' was substituted. I will continue to use the usual word with the understanding that I see it as a flexible, collaborative process. Some directors prepare a blocking of the whole play on paper in advance. They sometimes borrow the model box and invent moves for the whole company for every scene. To be honest, I find this almost impossible to do and in my experience it can lead to rather dull, stiff solutions. But on the other hand, I don't go into rehearsal with zero ideas about staging. You need to assess what you need to prepare in advance, what you are trying to achieve and then embark on rehearsals of the scene as a guide rather than a dictator or sergeant major.

For scenes with just two or three characters, I might decide on entrances in advance. Actors are really rather brilliant at blocking, so long as you set the context clearly and authoritatively. I wouldn't attempt to block the 'lovers lost in the wood' scenes in advance on paper, but in rehearsal I would approach them systematically by building up layer upon layer of knowledge of the scenes, sometimes just reading out loud and sometimes through 'blocking improvisations' which allow the actors themselves to explore the scene on their feet. I'll describe some of these later.

For larger scenes I will assess *where the power lies* in the scene from the narrative point of view and identify the most potent positions on the stage. I will work out *who is driving the scene*. In the opening scene, Theseus has the power and Egeus petitions him. Then the quarrel between Lysander and Demetrius crashes across everything. So who is driving the scene at any moment? I will make a note of the hierarchy of the characters. I will decide on entrances, or rather I will decide on what entrances I might start with. You must always be ready and willing to chuck out your first ideas the moment you see real human beings enacting your moves. I will revisit the work I did with my designer on axes.

You might consider **storyboarding** certain scenes, say this opening scene with Theseus, or the rehearsal in the forest or the Mechanicals' 'play within a play' at the end. It doesn't matter if you are a real duffer at drawing. The purpose is not to create a beautiful picture or a fixed image that you will then recreate onstage, but to force you to think visually and enter fully into a scene.

In the middle section of rehearsal you will need to address the **skills** needed to achieve your production. Do you need special choreography in the *Dream*, perhaps for the Bergamask at the end? Will you need help with the physical movement of the lovers in the wood? In *Henry V*, do you need a fight director? Remember there are safety issues that need addressing the moment that weapons or stage violence is employed. In my production, I started work with an eminent fight director, only to realize, quite early on, that there are in fact NO fights in *Henry V*. They talk about fighting a lot, but not a blow is struck onstage. Which is in itself an interesting dramaturgical feature. Ensure that you brief all your collaborators well in advance and forewarn stage management if particular rehearsal weapons or props are needed.

Nearly-at-the-end

The third phase of rehearsal is a learning, revisiting and consolidating time.

The key tool here is the **run through**. Plan your rehearsals to leave plenty of time for, ideally, several run throughs. On our imaginary three-week rehearsal period, you should be moving on to the third phase by the end of week two, or right at the start of week three.

Nearer the time, you will need to make a plan for technical rehearsals and previews with your technicians and your creative team.

Now you have a plan. So, let's go!

11

Rehearsing the Play: Beginning

The Rehearsal Room

In the following chapters we will explore the narrative of rehearsals, the journey of rehearsals from first day to opening night.

It's **Day One. You are walking down the road towards the rehearsal room**. You have conceptualized the rehearsals. Rehearsals have a beginning, a middle and a nearly-at-the-end.

You are nervous.

You've done your analysis, you've prepared the text, you've agreed a design, you've cast the play, you have a good stage management team.

You are very nervous.

You resolve to make the rehearsal room a constantly creative space. A hub of creative energy. Safe – always. Disciplined – most of the time. Focused – always.

Being nervous or even frightened is a perfectly normal, healthy state. My fear tends to last well into the rehearsal process, until I am comfortable with the cast and the production is alive and progressing. Just remember this: your preparation is your security and your cast and creative team want you to succeed. It's highly likely that your actors will feel as nervous as you.

So you're ready.

You enter the room.

You've checked it beforehand. It will be your home for the next three weeks, but essentially a place of work. In my career, I have worked in a whole variety of spaces. We created *A Doll's House* in a smelly room above a pub in Covent Garden; *Antony and Cleopatra* with Helen Mirren and Michael Gambon in a cramped scout hut (a location I reused for the Mechanicals scene in my film of *A Midsummer Night's Dream*); and too many church halls and community centres to remember.

You may not have any choice but, if possible, *find a room with plenty of space*; ideally with a bit of height and decent acoustics. Your room should have enough space to 'mark out' your set on the floor with tape. You are best to decide in advance which side of the room you will place yourself, in other words which side of the room will represent the 'fourth wall'. The positions of any walls on the set are marked out in coloured tape, a different colour for each act or movement. You may not want this done prior to rehearsals, your choice.

In the room there will be **props and furniture** which are substitutes for those you wish to use in your production. These should be as close to the real thing as possible, but if necessary, use three chairs as a sofa. Alternatively, you may decide to start rehearsals with an empty space and introduce furniture as you go along.

There should also be a **costume rail** upon which your stage management and designer can hang substitute costumes, garments or personal props. This is very important because many actors find it immensely helpful to rehearse in garments that feed and support their rehearsal process. Acting involves transformation and the right garment can help an actor move their centre closer to that of the character. For example a tight-fitting jacket and boots might help an actor create a military type. A long, heavy coat might help create a weighty character, like Lear. Many actors like to use practice skirts to rehearse in, especially if the production uses a period setting. Remember, these are *rehearsal garments* and need bear no resemblance to the final costume choices. They are used for purely pragmatic purposes: *Do they work? Do they help?* Hats can be useful. And gloves. Good, well-chosen rehearsal shoes can transform an actor's work. (Actors will often ask for the 'real' shoes to be provided as soon as possible.)

Identify a **wall** that can be used for research material, costume drawings, newspaper articles, ground plans, etc.

If possible, provide a second space where the actors can hang out, learn their lines, have coffee or chat.

You may have to compromise on all of the above, but this is the ideal.

Stage Management

You will have a support **stage management team**. Ideally this will consist of a **stage manager (SM)** who will 'run' the stage in the theatre and have overall responsibility. He/she will consult with you and organize the daily 'calls' so you get the right group of actors for each scene at the right time. On **Day One**, you will call the full company. For the read through and any accompanying presentation you might plan, other people might want to attend. In the professional theatre, this might include the wardrobe staff, press and publicity, perhaps your producer. In Tokyo I was greeted by not only the actors but all their agents as well! I tactfully banished them to an outer space. Remember, the rehearsal room is your space, it's a place of work and you can decide who has access and when. I would just advise tact, because all the support staff are also doing their jobs and it's easier, for example, to sell tickets for your show if they understand your vision. When you get to scene work or improvisations, clear the room of any but those directly involved. Rehearsal can be self-exposing and you and your actors have the right to work in private. You will have a **deputy stage manager (DSM)** who is 'on the book'. He/she will write down all the entrances and exits made by the actors, their positions onstage and moves they make, any changes you make to the text and will communicate any notes. For example, an actor may enter reading a letter; this will be noted and communicated to all relevant parties. The DSM will also be expected to give an actor prompts during rehearsal. The DSM is a key member of your team. *Stay close to him/her and keep them in the loop.* Make a habit of regularly asking them if there's any further information they need. There should also be an **assistant stage manager (ASM)** who will generally help out, but take particular care of the props and furniture in the rehearsal room.

Arrive in plenty of time so you can talk with stage management and greet people individually and generally be a good host. Following Max Beerbohm's definition: you may be a natural guest-like person, but on Day One of rehearsal, try your best to be a host-type person! It's good if there's coffee available, perhaps biscuits. Quite soon a warm atmosphere will develop. Choose the right moment and start the business of the day.

How do you begin the beginning?

There is an old adage that the purpose of the first day of rehearsal is to get to the second day. From a practical point of view, it's important that you *lead* the company on the first day. This will take the pressure off the actors and allow you to set the tone, set the agenda and create the kind of atmosphere that will be conducive to your kind of work. Stay in contact with all your actors throughout the day. Fear is deadly to creativity and human contact is the key to dispelling fear.

An Approach to Day One of Rehearsals

Here is a practical approach to Day One of rehearsals.

1 Sit everyone in a circle, preferable to an end-on schoolroom setup. Welcome them. Introduce everyone, or better still get everyone to introduce themselves.

2 Tell the company what this day means to you. Mark the moment. Make it special.

3 Make some introductory remarks about the play and your production. Talk about the movements of the play. Perhaps describe the artistic journey that has brought you to this point.

4 Introduce some of the research material you have accumulated. Keep plenty in reserve as it's hard for your group to absorb too much information at the beginning. At a later moment, pin this material on the wall.

5 Together with your designer, show the model of the set and talk through the play, movement by movement.

6 Introduce the costumes and explain the thinking behind them. Show the designs and then pin them on the wall. Some of your actors may want to discuss aspects of a design with you and your costume designer. Be alert to this.

7   **Read the play**, taking a coffee break at an appropriate point. Use the cut text and discourage detailed discussion about the choices you have made. You may want to reinstate some lines at a later point, or perhaps cut further. Actors respond in many, many different ways to a read through. Some actors arrive with a complete performance, worked out to the last detail. Some actors will give an inspiring rendition that will lift and excite the group. Less-experienced actors might feel that their talent is being judged. All actors will be curious about their fellow travellers on this journey. What sort of group is it? You, as director, will learn a lot about the dynamics of your cast. Observe but don't judge. Encourage your actors to *share* the text with the group in the circle rather than mumbling to themselves. Some directors use a technique whereby the text is read in a circle with each actor taking the next speech. This can help develop a collective response or ownership of the text and will curtail any single interpretation being imposed on the group. I have used this technique often, but beware; one in ten of the population in UK is thought to be dyslexic and for actors suffering from this disability, this exercise would be a nightmare. You or your stage management might discretely find out if anyone would find this particularly difficult.

8   Institute a general discussion, encouraging shy voices as well as confident contributors. During this discussion keep introducing your ideas and analysis. Encourage your actors to focus on the language of the play. Talk about the relationship of language to character and narrative. Ask questions that will develop understanding.

Examples:

Ask the actors to divide the play into three movements; compare this with your analysis.

Is there a moment or scene when your character could have made a different decision that would have altered the course of the play or their journey in the play? This is a useful exercise because it can reveal a 'hinge moment' for the actor. For example, Helena in the *Dream* might have decided *not* to pursue Hermia and Lysander into the forest. Her life would have followed a quite different path. This exercise can be particularly helpful to those with smaller parts; it helps them to share their creativity and gives their character status in the overall scheme of rehearsals.

Is there a line that pings out as being central to your character? Ask the same question after a week's work and then in the latter stages; has their perception altered/developed?

Ditto for the play. What line jumps out?

9 Start to reread the play, scene by scene, act by act, with you identifying important moments, ideas, themes and encouraging discussion. You can already start guiding and challenging the cast. They read a scene; ask them to reread it, playing a different or stronger action. (See Chapter 8, 'Awayday 2: Stanislavski and Actioning'). At this early stage of rehearsal, you can start pointing out how the 'plumbing' works. How this speech is driven by apposition or that speech has a long metaphor running right through it.

This will take you to the end of the first day at the very least. What a relief! You must be exhausted.

On the majority of productions, I would do most of the above, not necessarily in that order, but would take more than a single day. I would use the above template but would intersperse the 'table' work with work 'on our feet' and intersperse exercises with further discussion and analysis.

Let's take a pause here to talk through this 'off the text' work which I will loosely call **improvising**, a term I rarely use. **Let's take a mini Awayday** and connect ideas on improvisation directly to these early days of rehearsal.

12

Awayday 3: Improvisation

As a director you must consider every possible means of helping your cast to *identify* with their characters and *explore their actions and objectives*. Sitting down and talking about it will only get you so far; you need *practical* ways of engaging with an actor's emotions and imagination. This is where **improvisation** can help. So …

What is an improvisation? What is the point of an improvisation and how do I set about it?

An improvisation is any exercise in which the actor engages with a situation without using the text of the play you are rehearsing. **There are several aims:**

1 To help build a company from a group of individuals and to enable that company to develop trust and confidence in each other and themselves as part of the group. This can help rehearsals to run much more creatively and develop collective ownership of the project.
2 To help an actor build and identify with their character.
3 To enable the actor to develop their character in situations with and in relation to the other characters. In other

words to create, develop and explore relationships and to imaginatively enter the world of the play or production.**

4 **To explore scenes and situations in the play without using the text.**

Over recent years, improvisation has become part of the daily rehearsal life of many actors. It has been part of their training or they have used the techniques extensively at university or drama school. They feel comfortable and liberated. They may have a small part in the play but in an improvisation they have a fuller creative input. However, some actors feel it can be exposing in an unhelpful way. They don't fully understand the point of it. They feel that they can live freely and imaginatively inside the text and don't need to work off the text. Improvisation was not part of the training of many older actors and they feel vulnerable. They feel that some actors are witty and sharp, skilled and confident at improvisation, but might not be so hot when it comes to the text. I totally respect that and make judgements accordingly. Which is why I *never* use the word in rehearsal. I will use a whole spectrum of exercises, targeted to advance the rehearsal, frequently **non-verbal exercises**, a valid form of improvisation and mostly unthreatening. Most important of all, you need to lead your cast in a clear, confident manner, **setting out any rules or parameters before beginning**.

Building a Company

This is particularly true of the first of the above categories, **building a company**. You may have in your rehearsal room students from different colleges or faculties, who have never even met before. They will be nervous, excited. You may have a group of actors some of whom have worked together professionally over many years. I have had groups of opera singers who have quite literally flown in from across the world. On almost every production I direct, in drama and opera, I will get the actors on their feet on the very first day. This may start with a simple **warm up**, ideally both physical and vocal. You don't have to be an expert at it. Just loosen the body and the voice. You may be lucky enough to have a movement director on your production or a choreographer to help with this. But I tend to do this work myself. We will stretch, we will shake, we will bend. We will go through the vowels. We will articulate the consonants. We will try some tongue twisters. You can have music playing if you want.

Or I will skip any warm up and simply get the actors to **move in the space**. Identify the space they should use; an uncluttered empty space, perhaps marked out by four chairs. They can move anywhere they like, randomly, but not touching each other. No talking. They can make eye contact. I will add in simple instructions: stop, move; slowly, quicker; stop; move; stop; move quicker. No bumping into each other, but become *expert* at near misses! I will ask them to practise stopping *perfectly* like statues and without any extraneous movement. They should be still and concentrated. Now move around again. We will practise this several times. We will practise forming a perfect circle on a sudden instruction. Now move around again. Each actor will silently chose another actor in the group and subtly pick up their rhythms. We will create a single rhythm within the group listening to each other's footsteps while walking around. You may hand on the initiative from one actor to another; better still set them a task to subtly pass on the lead from one to another without talking. All this may sound pretty simple stuff, but it's invaluable early on in rehearsals. You will learn a lot about your group and they will get to know each other. Don't linger too long on this stage. Your instinct will tell you when to move onto exercises designed to **help your actors build their characters**.

Building a Character

This is not a mysterious process, although the results can often be quite magical. You simply set exercises that allow the actors to *identify* with their characters. **This process works from the inside out.** As we have seen, **the text will work on the actor from the outside in**. You can start very simply with the actor walking around the room **as the character**. Again, no talking. Repeat this a couple of times. The alchemy will start working. The process of identification. Remember this is *private* work undertaken in public. Warn the actors not to *demonstrate* their characters. They don't need to show you anything. Or discuss what they're doing. You don't need to see any difference at all; it's what's going on inside the actor that counts. It's the *ignition of the imagination that counts*. I might ask the actors to choose an adjective that seems right for their character and walk around, trying it on like an internal garment. Better still, choose a snatch of a song that expresses your character. This can be sung out loud. Or a line of poetry. Encourage empiricism; trial and error. If that song doesn't work, try something else. How does that fit?

You can develop this work logically without adding too much contextual information. Your character cleans his/her shoes, brushes his/her hair, puts on a scarf. In other words you add a ***physical*** dimension to the exercise. You can then develop this into a ***situation***. Your character puts on his/her coat and scarf in order to go to the shops; in order to meet a friend for coffee; in order to attend an important interview. I would start discussing some of these exercises with the actors. How was that? Did you believe it? How might it relate to the story? Try again. But don't dwell too long in chat!

The use of simple, ready-to-hand props and furniture can prove highly effective. They can help to root the character. When I directed Cheryl Campbell as Nora in Ibsen's *A Doll's House*, we provided a whole room with chairs, tables, cups, saucers, clothes, props of every description; she spent hours in that space on her own, working with the props and furniture, creating the physical and imaginative life of Nora. From the private work she did alone, she built a fully realized human being that underwent Nora's journey every night for nearly two years, and en route won every acting award going!

Early on in rehearsals, start raiding the costume rail, trying improvisations with this hat or that jacket. In a way, this is similar to children using a dressing up box. It can be fun but often very revealing. *External accoutrements impact and nourish an actor's inner life.*

In the early stages of rehearsal, I often use exercises that will stretch the imagination. Sophocles' *Theban* plays, which we staged in the Swan Theatre, Stratford-upon-Avon, provided quite severe challenges and seemed to require a different approach. The subject matter touched on the very frontiers of our experience and our actors had to make that journey. So, with my choreographer Sue Lefton, we devised a different approach. Some of the exercises involved mask work, in this case using big brown paper bags with holes for eyes and mouth. Much of the work I have found applicable to my work on Shakespeare. Examples: your character arrives at a hilltop and sees a view. Or arrives at the ocean's edge. Perhaps they see a sailing boat in the far distance. Perhaps that boat contains a friend. How do they feel? Repeat the exercise. The whole company is still watching. I encourage the actors to express what they feel physically and vocally.

Do they want to stretch out? Or let out a cry or a sigh? You can turn the gas up: the boat contains a parting lover who's going away for six months. You should repeat such exercises to allow the actor to build a sensory/emotional memory of a situation. You might want to tie in the exercise to a moment in the play. Remember, the stage actor has to repeat his/her performance night after night.

In Chekov's *The Cherry Orchard* I started to use **'gates'** and have used them in my work ever since. By 'gates' I mean two chairs set 1-2 metres apart. The whole company can watch the process and try the exercise one at a time. An actor can walk through the gate and behold! The Pacific Ocean! Or behold! The muddy landscape near to the village of Agincourt. Or behold! The Forest of Arden! Gates are particularly useful to explore the emotional memory bank that each one of us carries around with him/her. So an actor can walk through the gate and discover or recreate a particular potent memory that drives and defines a character. This can be quite basic; walk through the gates and recreate a special joyous moment for the character. Perhaps the moment when Hermia receives the first love letter from Lysander. Encourage particularity. What does the room look like? What time of day? No words allowed, no props. Don't create a scene, don't demonstrate. Or a sad moment. Hermia, create the moment when you hear that your Mother has passed away. Penelope Wilton, playing Madame Ranevskaya in *The Cherry Orchard*, used gates to create for herself the loss of her son Grisha who drowned before the play begins. She walked through and stood quite still. Then her body contorted in silent grief. She used this very action in the play when she encountered and embraced Trofimov, her dead son's tutor, whom she had not seen for many years. Actors will often use memories or events from their own lives as 'triggers' to enable a memory or moment for the character. In the same production, all the actors were asked to find potent childhood memories that might give access to the character or help to make a foundation, a reality for the character. One after the other they passed through the gates and they created a memory. The company looked on. Sometimes they would repeat it by walking through the gates again. Trial and error! Then we discussed what had happened. Grandmothers featured heavily in the moments chosen and, fascinatingly, so did smells. I didn't know whether the memories were of the actors or the characters. They were all triggers. The collection of memories, created and shared, contributed massively to a shared sense of purpose and identity that lasted through the Stratford run, the West End run and right through the national tour.

Developing Relationships and Exploring the World of the Play

This work can segue straight out of the work explored in the above section and can swiftly feed into the themes of the play and nourish the important relationships. Try to explore the world of the play 'on your feet' and not just sitting around. Again, start with non-verbal encounters. Ask your actors to walk around the room as their characters, this time encountering the other characters, making eye contact, but not speaking or touching. Encourage concentration; be aware that occasionally one actor might be less engaged than the others and can easily spoil it for the group. You would be wise to tactfully deal with this. Early on in rehearsal, you might ask the group to respect each other's working methods. Such and such an exercise might not be working for you, but it might be for everyone else.

As the group moves around, you can quickly add information. Ask them to increase awareness of their **relationship to other characters**.

Imagine you are directing *Romeo and Juliet*. You would prompt your actors. Who's playing your father? Your mother? Your cousin? What do you feel about each of those relations? Make eye contact with your friends. Who is your best friend? Who is your character attracted to? Make contact with Friar Lawrence. What do you feel about him? Does your character despise another character? The play is set in a divided almost tribal society. Familial enmities were common in Medieval Italian cities with rival factions of Guelphs and Ghibellines. Leonard Bernstein relocated the play to Hell's Kitchen in New York for his musical *West Side Story*, with rival gangs of Italians and Puerto Ricans. As your group moves in the space, ask them to be aware of rival families. Still no talking. Give one gang a piece of torn rag or a handkerchief that they tuck in at the back of their jeans or at the back of their collars, so their rivals will know who is who. They move in the space, avoiding physical contact but focusing their dislike on the other gang. You might try one group trying to steal the handkerchief from another without bodily contact and without the 'victim' knowing about it. This variation would be best tried in smaller groups. Gather each group at separate ends of the room. Ask an actor from each group to cross the room and pass their 'rival'. Watch the body language. Montague might be courteous but cool to Capulet; Tybalt might be provocative to everyone; Sampson might be downright rude. Keep adding in specific information that relates to your production. Why, in the world of *your* production do the Capulets despise the Montagues? In many respects, theses exercises are games, but like all good games, they allow you to explore real, sometimes dangerous, emotions in a controlled and safe manner.

Try a contrasting exercise. Make them *physicalize* these relationships. I do this first by a **group sculpture**. I would ask a key figure, Juliet's father Capulet, to sit on a chair in the middle of the space. One by one, I ask the actors to make a *living sculpture* that expresses their relationship and how they feel about this character. Encourage the actors to be abstract rather than literal. To express their inner feelings. So Juliet might sit curled on his knee, or lie flat on the floor with her head on his feet. There you have two totally different relationships of father to daughter. Each actor joins one after the other. Romeo might put his head on Juliet's lap. Friar Lawrence might stand behind Capulet looking down. Montague might stand with his back to Capulet. I would then discuss the sculpture and the choices made. You can repeat the exercise with the Friar as the central character, or the two lovers. It is also important to make clear at which point in the story the exercise takes place. Relationships evolve and change after the murder of Tybalt. In between exercises you should keep feeding in ideas about how this work might relate to your production and your research into the world of the play. For example you could talk about Elizabethan ideas of marriage; to what degree would they be love matches and to what degree financial arrangements or dynastic couplings. Perhaps you have identified a passage from a book of social history; read it aloud or get an actor to read it aloud.

You can go one stage further and try to measure the shift in relationships through the course of the play. Here's a simple exercise. Gather the group in a big circle and ask them to move to the character who, at the beginning of the play, their character *thinks about most*. Perhaps put their hand on his/her shoulder. Some interesting choices will emerge. So Tybalt thinks about Juliet the most? He thinks about Romeo the most? Discuss the choices. Now do the same exercise for the end of the play. Discuss the journey the character has made.

There are hundreds of variations on these exercises. What I would encourage is a working method that is less table bound, more inclusive, freer. After a certain exercise, you might want to sit everyone down and read some poems that strike you as important or show some photographs. And I do not do all of this work on every production I direct. When I directed David Suchet as Lady Bracknell in Wilde's *Importance of being Earnest*, we did some useful work on our feet, but with the particular cast I had assembled, it seemed right to move quite quickly into staging work.

As described with *Romeo and Juliet*, I try to invent exercises that allow the actors to explore their emotions and the intensity of their feelings. In the *Dream* there is a long sequence of scenes in the middle movement when the lover's emotions are muddled and intensified by Puck's interference. I directed the play at Stratford in the 1990s. We played London, toured the UK, a Coast to Coast in America, Broadway, a world tour and made a feature film. I had several changes of cast and had the challenge of keeping the production fresh over several years. We used a simple exercise. At the beginning, Hermia loves Lysander. So I had these two actors move in the space and explore their feelings, but without touching or speaking. Then I might turn up the gas a bit: they love each other *very much*. Then I would add in Demetrius, who also loves Hermia, but does not like Lysander. Still no touching or speaking. And then Helena. I would keep on increasing the emotional temperature, so that each is *desperately* in love with another. Now change the brief, the 'who loves who', following Puck's interventions. Chaos quickly develops. As a result of these exercises, the actors built a visceral connection to the events of the play and many of the moves and situations that emerged were incorporated into the final 'blocking' of the scenes.

With a Shakespeare play, it is important to establish the relative **status** of each character right from the start. Shakespeare's world was much more structured, more hierarchical than ours and we need to understand that to penetrate his world. This is true even if you are planning to set the play in the present day. An appreciation of the relative status of characters will help you make logical and creative choices. Remember, status is not an absolute state, it is *relative*. So there is hierarchy in Pistol's group of East End lads as much as in the upper reaches of Henry's court. There are dozens of status games you can explore, whole bookfulls! You can hand out playing cards and ask the group to move around and relate according to the 'number' you are given, keeping your own card hidden. That's quite fun because you don't know the value of the card allotted to another actor. What quickly emerges is that status is not just a function of your social position and therefore how you carry yourself but also of the way you are treated by your fellows and how they behave towards you. At the end of this exercise, ask the group to form a line; high cards on the left, low cards on the right. It's likely that it's pretty evident who had the highest and lowest cards; it's the middle orders that are revealing. I will then ask the company to form this line with the characters in the play. With *Henry V*, I might do the French and the English separately. This will lead to some very interesting discussion. What is the hierarchy amongst the aristocrats? You may find you need further research here. Get one of the actors to do this and come back with his/her findings. What is the hierarchy amongst soldiers? So the world of the play is discussed, but in an active, non-academic way.

Now ask your actors, in their 'status' positions, to try to articulate the **values** of the characters. What is most important to you? What do you care about most? Your country? Your family? Your friends? Ask them to finish a sentence beginning 'I want ...'. Develop the situation. Are you content with your lot? Where in this line up do *you* see yourself, not where society has placed you. Get everyone to move to *their* choice of status in life. This will open up really important discussion and help set the agenda for further work. Be prepared for the actors to make unexpected choices and be prepared to run with these ideas if you think they are valid, or challenge them if not. This might be the moment to introduce the idea of **life histories**. I never ask my actors to write out their character's CVs, that seems a bit like school. But I do regularly challenge them on details of biography. Where were you born? When did you meet, say, Pistol? What might your education have consisted of? These questions will often lead to further exploration that can enrich the group's knowledge of the world of the play. Prepare for these conversations and do the necessary research.

In some Shakespeare plays, there are **master and servant** relationships. Think of King Lear and his Fool or the Antipholus's and Dromios in *The Comedy of Errors*. These relationships are almost non-existent in modern Western society, but are crucial to the mechanics of these plays. The Fool in *Lear* is described as 'all licens'd' but everyone seems to have the right to beat him! You will find it very constructive to spend time with these actors improvising their relationship. This can be done simply with the 'master' giving instructions to the 'servant'. 'Arrange those chairs for me', 'Get me a coffee', 'Clean my shoes'. Or silently, which also works. Servants invariably get things wrong and the resultant incompetence or misunderstanding can be the source of much comedy. In the Italian Commedia dell'arte tradition, this is taken to extremes, even high art, with the servant scoring points off the master behind his/her back, often with the collusion of the audience. I took this Shakespearean/Italian connection to the extreme in my *Comedy of Errors*, and used clown faces and elaborate, brilliant comic routines between master and servants. When Antipholus arrives home to find his front door barred by his wife, we invented a whole *mise en scène*, using a free-standing door, complete with handle and letterbox. It had to be constantly held upright by one of the performers, but offered fantastic opportunities. At one point Dromio bent down to shout through the letterbox, the door flipped over his back and he stood up on the opposite side of the divide, apparently having disappeared from the sight of 'his' Antipholus. He bent down a second time and, flip, ended up where he started.

Exploring Scenes and Situations in the Play without Using the Text

As rehearsals develop, you can explore situations in the play and relevant contextual situations through improvisation. These have the benefit of your company making shared discoveries about the play and enriching and enlightening the story. They can be quite simple, for example the first meeting of Romeo and Juliet in their own words, not using Shakespeare's text, or elaborate set ups involving the whole company. In all circumstances, make the situation and the rules clear beforehand. Confine the space within the rehearsal room or you might find some of your cast taking off to the local Starbucks. If possible, use real objects or good substitutes rather than mime. Define the situation as clearly as possible; time of day, place, etc.

To be honest, I rarely use improvisation to explore a situation in the play 'off the text' and never early on in rehearsal, before the actor has built up a familiarity with the character. I find the kind of work described in the earlier sections much more beneficial. There's a philosophical point to be made here which underpins the practical. Shakespeare's language is 'heightened'. His characters do not talk like you and me. Their experiences are frequently more extraordinary than yours or mine. Their thoughts more complex and finer. And so your actors need **to grow into the character**, expand into the character, not reduce the character down to our mundane experiences. There is, crucially, a common ground of emotion, intellectual discovery and spiritual experience shared by all humanity and it's your job and that of your actors to make those experiences, those connections, those bridges accessible. Sometimes the way to do this is to create a situation that is contemporary and real. So Romeo and Juliet might meet for the first time in a bar or a club. My question to you is, given the actors you are working with, is it best for them to meet in a bar using Shakespeare's words or to improvise their own. Perhaps both.

I will, however, improvise the *blocking* and the *situation*, using Shakespeare's words and I find this enormously creative. I'll discuss this in detail later when we get onto staging the play.

I do sometimes make large improvisations that can open up the canvas of a production or have the benefit of coalescing a company. These can happen early on in rehearsal. These can fizz up the atmosphere of a scene, feed in ideas for staging and will certainly help the actors playing smaller parts. Let's take an example. The ball scene in *Romeo and Juliet*. This can involve the whole company. Lay on some good dance music, organize some water for wine, set out the rules and parameters and state the situation precisely. With a big improvisation, give it a clear structure. Perhaps have three movements. Movement one: setting up the party, involving the Capulets, their servants and close friends. Movement two: the arrival of Juliet. Perhaps she has a special scarf to wear. Get one of the servants to organize a good track of music for her arrival. Section three: the arrival of Mercutio, Romeo and their pals. I would advise you orchestrate these movements, like a conductor, and decide when to move forward. Give Juliet and Mercutio a cue. Then let the improvisation run. Afterwards, there will be masses to discuss, lots of lessons learnt and ideas to be pinched and incorporated into the final production.

Choosing a big public or semi-public situation will certainly provide you with an exciting canvass that will provide energy and opportunity. At the beginning of rehearsals for *Twelfth Night* in Tokyo, we undertook a long improvisation around the death and mourning of Olivia's brother. They created a Japanese style wake and the rehearsal extended over a whole morning. It was fascinating for me because I did not know any of the actors and had not worked in Japan before. The formality of the situation played to their strengths and I gained a wonderful insight into Japanese custom and manners.

On the first day of my *Winter's Tale* rehearsals I provided a big bag of pasta and tomatoes and asked them to make a feast. It turned into a party! Pretend wine was drunk, tables were danced on, stories were told. They achieved something *together*. A group became a company and they toured together in towns and villages across the land in the dark days of the 1984 miner's strike.

13

Rehearsing the Play: End of the Beginning

Work on Language

Let's get back to our narrative, beginning, middle and nearly-at-the end.

Always intersperse work 'on your feet' with text work. This doesn't need to be round a table; you can stand up with scripts in hand or sit around on cushions. You will almost certainly find a wide range of **language skills**. The best way to achieve a collective approach to Shakespeare's language is firstly for you to take a strong lead and be clear about what you want; and secondly to work iteratively, relating character development to the plumbing, to 'how he does it', and to Stanislavskian analysis. For example, when you read the Westmoreland/Henry scene ('What's he that wishes so?'), point out the way Henry pushes through to the ends of the lines. The urgency of the situation is there in the verse, for free. The actor will be able to connect that characteristic of language to Henry's character. Is he impulsive? Manipulative? A brilliant speaker? Don't be afraid to keep emphasizing 'appositions' – it's how the character thinks, how the argument develops. Or 'follow the metaphor right through' and 'finish the thought'. Or 'use the alliteration', it will empower you.

When I first joined the RSC, there were 'sonnet classes' in the lunch hours. These were voluntary but mostly well attended. Each actor learnt a Shakespeare sonnet off by heart from a prescribed selection. The atmosphere was relaxed and the director, usually Terry Hands or John Barton, would lead the discussion. Sonnets were chosen because they contain most of the salient characteristics of Shakespeare's language, in miniature. They have the added advantage of not being drawn from *x* or *y*'s role in the production and so we were on neutral territory. Over the weeks, a collective approach to the language emerged.

You will need to decide on a strategy. I would certainly announce upfront that you want to develop a collective approach to the language. You may want to try more formal sessions, which can be great fun, especially if the group is not too large. The key is learning together. Whatever you do, avoid a classroom approach; this will certainly turn people off!

Work on Character

In your opening period of rehearsal, it is important to **allow time to discuss character** with each actor. This can be done 'on your feet', as part of a discussion about a particular exercise or improvisation. It can be done 'at table', addressing each actor in turn with full company present. Or it can be done one on one, if you have the time.

I prefer a mixture of all three. Allow private time if possible, but a shared approach can be beneficial, as one actor's choice or inspiration can affect another. This is especially true of a particular grouping within the play, such as the Mechanicals in the *Dream*. This is a group of characters who clearly know each other very well, perhaps meet regularly at the pub or even for amateur theatricals. One actor's ideas will spark off another's. So in the *Dream*, I would call this group together for discussion and character work. Likewise the Fairies.

As a point of departure, I follow basic Stanislavskian methodology. Who are you and what do you want? You can introduce *actioning* and *objectives* at this stage of rehearsal.

Always start from the text. What information is given? With the Mechanicals, we know their trades and we know they are familiar with each other. There is a hierarchy within the group. We know that Bottom is familiar with a certain bombastic acting style (the 'raging rocks' speech). Where did he encounter this? At the theatre, presumably. What actors has he seen? Perhaps he saw Richard Burbage? Or Edward Alleyn in *Tamburlaine* perhaps. Encourage your actors to make connections across the centuries. Are there any performers nowadays whose style correlates? Or singers? Freddie Mercury perhaps? It's important that the actor's imagination is stimulated by these discussions.

I will sometimes set tasks or projects. I might ask the actor playing Friar Lawrence to prepare a short presentation on religious instruction, so the whole group gets a sense of the importance of the church in their society. In order to fulfil this brief, they will need to know the world in which you are setting the play. Does the Friar do formal Sunday school? Or does he run the local disco? Or both?

I've always been reluctant to ask for full **biographies** of characters. It smacks of school homework. But try to find *imaginative* ways of unlocking character. Perhaps ask each actor to choose a piece of poetry their character particularly likes. Or choose their character's desert island discs and relate each piece of music to an imaginary event or person in their character's life. (*Desert Island Discs* is a BBC radio programme where a guest chooses their favourite pieces of music.) Or ask for a photo or an image that engages them. Stick it on the wall.

You will arrive at a point when you need to move on to scene work, from beginning to middle. It's important to recognize this moment and react to it. I have known directors to sit their casts around table for well over a week, by which time rehearsals feel like school and the natural energy of actors has dissipated.

So you are ready to move on …

14

Rehearsing the Play: Middle

This section of rehearsal will take you up to your first run through. This chapter will explore how to conduct detailed scene work, how to block scenes and how to further develop characterizations.

First things first.

Your stage manager will want to have your call for the following day by lunchtime at the latest, so he/she can work out the logistics and work out any calls that other departments might want to make. For example, wardrobe might want Hermia for a costume fitting. Ideally, you would plan your calls two or three days in advance, although I'm often rather lax about this. You will have to make a judgement about how much time to allot each scene. This begs the question of rhythm, how fast or slow do you want to proceed? My personal preference is to go quite quickly through the play as a first pass, leaving plenty of time to revisit everything a second time more thoroughly. I find this allows the actors to get a clearer idea of the architecture of their roles. Alternatively, there may be scenes that require detailed work from the get-go, so use a varied rhythm.

You must also decide which actors to call for a particular scene. For first rehearsal, do you just call the actors who speak, or call every actor who will eventually be in the scene? This is partly a question of rhythm; if you are moving quickly, you might just call speakers and involve the others at a second stage. Although you are reluctant to waste people's time, a full group engenders a fuller emotional investment in a scene. Your call.

Aims for Middle Section of Rehearsal

Let's imagine you are halfway through week one, about to embark on your next phase. You want to achieve:

- **A deeper sense of the meaning of each scene and the shape and drive of each scene.**
- **A deeper sense of character and relationships.**
- **A first blocking of each scene.**
- **Work on the language as an iterative, ongoing agenda, always trying to integrate language with motivation, with action.**
- **Work on any special skills needed for your show** (e.g. choreography, fights, acrobatics, etc.).

Examples from *Romeo and Juliet*

Let's take the opening of *Romeo and Juliet* as our example. The play starts off with a Prologue, a Chorus (if you haven't decided to cut it!). Do you assign this speech to a special 'Chorus' character, dressed perhaps as a townsperson, or in modern dress? Or allot the part to a neutral party like Friar Lawrence or the Prince? An alternative, which I like, is to make this speech genuinely 'choral' and divide the lines amongst the whole company. This communicates that we, the company, are telling a story over which we have ownership. The full company create a relationship with the audience straightaway. Scholars of Greek tragedy believe that the chorus lies at the very beginning, is the first heart beat of drama. Then out of the chorus stepped an actor, the first actor, the protagonist, followed by the second actor, the antagonist, and so dramatic conflict was born. In my own work, I have sought out a choral framework to several of Shakespeare's play, notably *Cymbeline*, *The Winter's Tale* and *Pericles*, the great romantic plays of his later years. A collective 'storytelling' device was highly effective.

If I opted for a single actor, what are my options? He/she walks on and talks directly to the house. Simple. Or you can create a *context*. The light goes up onto an armchair in which is seated a friar who turns to the audience and speaks. Perhaps he is working on his potions and remedies. Or a character walks on carrying the evening newspaper which has reported on the deaths you are about to witness. Or have a TV news crew filming the Prologue, perhaps with a screen with a live feed. Each of these options will create a different relationship with the audience, a different angle.

If you opt for the choral approach, how should you tackle it? Firstly, make a provisional distribution of lines, reserving the right to reallocate as work progresses. Then assign entrances. They enter the space and, when assembled, commence the speech. This is an important lesson: try to resist dreaming up the perfect formation or blocking onstage, then working backwards to achieve it. Let them enter in their own manner and watch and listen. I guarantee something interesting and surprising will happen. They may spread out equidistantly or gather in a single tight group or several clusters. What feels exciting?

At this point, start intervening, directing. Work empirically, trial and error. Should they enter with urgency or with the weight of grief in their hearts? Try both. Watch the results. They will quite soon ask you who they are. Characters from the play? Working people? Actors? What costume should I wear? All valid questions that will affect how they enter and how they gather. The work you have done in the space, company building and character development, will immediately pay off. You will find your actors have an increased spacial awareness and will feel comfortable trying out different stagings.

Let's move on to Act 1 Scene 1. You will have labelled it already, perhaps 'The Rumble'. For convenience, you should divide the scene into 1A, 1B, 1C, etc., so the actors aren't hanging around. Let's say 1A covers the scene up to Benvolio's entrance, so you start off with the speakers, Sampson, Gregory and Abraham and perhaps their gangs, the Montagues and the Capulets.

Reread the scene a couple of times standing in the space rather than sitting down. Have a quick, sharp discussion about the situation, character and relationships within each group. Have they grown up together? Who is top dog? Why?

At this point, as a warm up, I would revisit one or two of the exercises that I described earlier. As they move, they should form into gangs. Again, no words, no touching. With each exercise, turn up the emotional gas, increase the stakes. I would then ask the actors to play the scene through with Shakespeare's text. I would give them entrances and then allow the scene to run. This process is very important for actors; to play the scene freely once or twice without too much directorial input.

The Tank

Before setting about staging or blocking any scene, I might try the following exercise. It is particularly useful for exploring quite dense texts and will help to physically free up your cast and provide invaluable insights into a scene. I have used it with students, experienced actors and world-renowned opera singers. I call it the **tank**.

Make a circle of ten to fifteen chairs, facing inwards, no gaps between chairs. This is your **tank** (Figure 4). You ask your actors to play the scene inside the tank, as fully and dynamically as possible with the following rules:

1   If you are in a scene, or even onstage without any lines, you are *in* the tank. When your character exits, you *leave* the tank.

2   When you are in the tank *you must be seated* whenever possible. No standing in the middle talking.

3   When you move, you must *move directly to another chair* and sit down.

4   You should make a move to another chair with *a change of thought or an emotional change or a change in the direction the character takes.*

5   *You do not need to be speaking to make a move.* You can move at any time you like. You can move as a *reaction to another character*. For example, character A in a scene might say to character B: ' I hate you!' Character B might move to a chair as far away as possible. Character A might pursue him/her across the tank to ram home the insult.

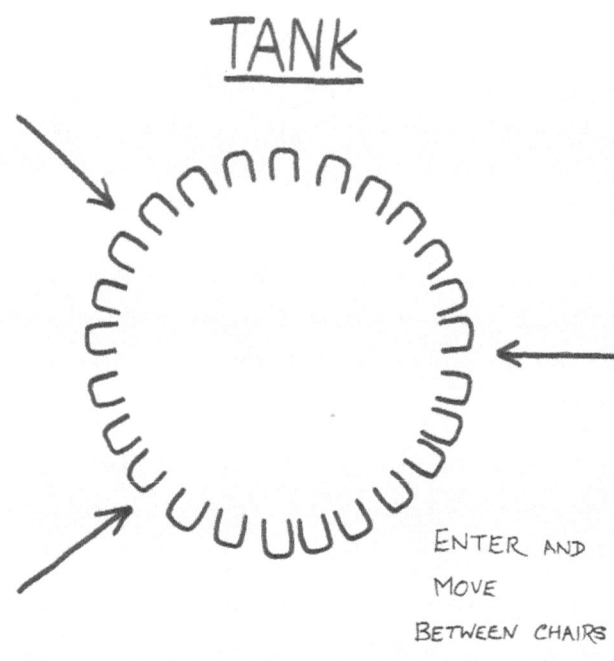

Figure 4 Tank. Drawing courtesy of Adrian Noble.

6 Remember, this is not a naturalistic exercise. The aim is to express and physicalize thought and emotion. Encourage your actors to be bold: move first, think and analyse afterwards.

This exercise can work with monologues and with scenes with many characters. There is no right way or wrong way. It is an exploration. For clarity, let's look at the opening lines of our old friend Hamlet's famous speech.

> HAMLET
> To be, or not to be, that is the question,
> Whether 'tis nobler in the mind to suffer
> The slings and arrows of outrageous fortune,
> Or to take arms against a sea of troubles,
> And by opposing end them? To die: to sleep;
> No more; and by a sleep to say we end
> The heart-ache and the thousand natural shocks
> That flesh is heir to, 'tis a consummation
> Devoutly to be wish'd. To die, to sleep;
> To sleep: perchance to dream.
>
> (*Hamlet* 3.1.58–67)

You ask your actor to enter, to sit down and to *move* on every change of thought or emotion. He/she might want to move just one chair to the side for a small change of thought or right across the tank for a big change. I will mark the points where an actor might move with this symbol: <<

> To be, << or not to be, << that is the question,<<
> Whether 'tis nobler in the mind to suffer
> The slings and arrows of outrageous fortune,<<
> Or to take arms against a sea of troubles,
> And by opposing end them?<<To die: <<to sleep;<<
> No more; << and by a sleep to say we end
> The heart-ache and the thousand natural shocks
> That flesh is heir to, << 'tis a consummation

Devoutly to be wish'd. To die, << to sleep;
To sleep: << perchance to dream.

There's no right way or wrong way. Here, I have suggested eleven possible moves. That's a lot! By physicalizing changes of thought, this will help you and your actor to appreciate how Hamlet thinks. It's not contemplative and laid back, but active and dynamic. You would certainly not want your Hamlet to replicate these moves onstage, but he/she should take forward the *energy*. Without question, this exercise works best if the actors are 'off the book', in other words know their lines off by heart. But it will always yield something and will sometimes suggest a complete staging for a scene.

I used this exercise at the Aix en Provence Festival when I was directing Monteverdi's *Il Ritorno d'Ulisse in Patria*. It begins with a long, complex, highly emotional scene between Penelope and her companion. We played this scene, first with the words spoken and then sung, in the orchestra pit of the theatre, our 'tank' with chairs arranged as above. When they had finished, the singers immediately played the scene on the stage. I only suggested entrances. The blocking that the performers created that first rehearsal was *perfect* and became the staging for the final production and its many revivals.

I used this exercise to enable the last great scene in Ibsen's *Brand* when the eponymous character takes to the mountains, pursued by the whole town. I assembled as many chairs as possible in a great circle; the whole company was in the tank, speakers, non-speakers alike. As Ralph Fiennes (Brand) moved or spoke or provoked them, each character moved, sometimes together, sometimes separately. As the scene hotted up, the frequency and size of the moves increased. In many ways it was chaotic, but it opened up this most difficult scene and, at the same time, allowed every single actor to explore and animate their individual thoughts and actions.

So with my opening scene of *Romeo and Juliet,* I would use this exercise and then immediately ask the actors to play the scene freely and improvise the moves. You will find that 50 per cent of the blocking of the scene is done for you! Wherever possible, allow the blocking to evolve naturally, perhaps using some of the work described above. Remember, your actors are *inside* the characters and will have good instincts about where to place themselves in relation to other characters and when to move and why. Their instincts will develop as their understanding and empathy with their character deepens and so be prepared to modify your choices from rehearsal to rehearsal. It's an iterative process. I always remind young directors that actors don't stop working when you leave the room or move on to another scene; they carry on discussing, trying things out, making suggestions to each other. Have the confidence to embrace these activities. Your job is partly to enable and harness their natural instincts and partly to edit, shape and present.

Blocking

Here are **some considerations for blocking a scene**.

1. What is the **style** of the play? In other words, how does the material relate to the audience? Let's look at an extreme contrast. A naturalistic drama like Arnold Wesker's *Roots* is a quite different animal to Aeschylus' *Oresteia*. The style of the former requires a detailed, almost cinematic, replication of everyday life; the latter requires a stylistic choice that will

enlighten and transport the audience, that will make logical the events and the dramatic devices of the author. In this case, the style is predicated upon the fact that the *Oresteia* was written to be performed in masks. An actor will move and relate to audience quite differently if he/she is masked. The wearing of masks can trigger emotional release and significant changes of behaviour; you only have to witness the Venice Carnival to appreciate this. In mask work, I have found that the performer loses power if he/she turns their face/mask away from the audience or into profile. It's as if a light is switched off. So a masked actor will instinctively relate to the other characters in a quite different way to the characters in a naturalistic drama.

A Shakespeare play is not a naturalistic text and in some ways it is helpful to think of it as a masked drama. Only in this case, *the mask is the language* and not a face covering. I find I need to keep the language alive and in constant touch with the audience, or the light will go out. This does not mean that your actors must face front all the time, but your blocking has to constantly *triangulate* the action, character to character to audience.

The text of *Roots*, brilliantly crafted by Wesker, persuades us that we are witnessing real events, and the actor's craft is to inhabit the characters and those events in real, recognizable space. The blocking of a **naturalistic play** like *Roots* is therefore predicated upon the physical elements of the room: the doors, the windows, the furniture, etc. Typically, in a proscenium theatre, the audience would look in at the world through the *fourth wall*. Such a naturalistic event can take place in the round as well as 'end on'.

Some very exciting discoveries have been made by switching or substituting styles. For example, some directors have presented Greek Chorus's in a completely naturalistic way. And Sarah Kane, led by the example of Edward Bond, has ritualized naturalistic behaviour and shed a new, cruel, unsentimental light on our contemporary world. In cinema, Lars von Trier made a stylistic somersault in the film *Dogville*, forcing us to re-examine that most realistic of media.

2. What is the **situation**? Is the scene interior or exterior? Public or private? Day or night? Our opening scene from *Romeo and Juliet* moves from private to public. It can be played as an interior or an exterior. If it is an interior, is there a window or another light source? If exterior where is the sun, the prominent light known as the key light? Such details help to define the space.

3. Do you need **furniture**? A chair or table or bench can often provide focus and counterpoint. So in the opening court scene of *Henry V*, a throne onstage will give context and support the narrative. The subject of the scene is power, here represented by a throne. Does Henry sit on it? If so, when? How do the noblemen in this hierarchical society relate to it? By the way, a throne does not need to be a reproduction of a great Medieval object. You can put an old kitchen chair onstage and call it a throne. Your actors can *endow* it with respect and authority and it will serve the same function of facilitating the blocking of the scene. Indeed, the substitution of the everyday for the formal can have startling results. In a late rehearsal of *Titus Andronicus* at Bristol Old Vic, Pete Postlethwaite couldn't find the gory severed head he was supposed to carry on,

so grabbed a nearby fire bucket and presented that instead. Amazing!

In my production of *Richard III*, I used a long council table with chairs, placed laterally across the stage, with an upstage centre entrance for the scene leading to the arrest and execution of Hastings. We gained huge political significance from the to-ings and fro-ings from the table, like a high-powered board meeting or a scene from *Succession*.

You can use furniture in a quite realistic manner and this can provide immediate and potent blocking solutions. For example, you might set the opening scene of *Romeo and Juliet* in a crowded cafe, in Italy or Soho or New York, populated with your whole cast as waiters and customers. It can be interior or exterior, private at a single table, then open out to a public scene. You can delineate space with light or even with quality of movement (Sampson and Gregory in real time, other customers in slo-mo). The tables and chairs will prove mighty useful to your fight director when the rumble starts and you are trying to create chaos. The confined space will immediately define your blocking choices and add focus and heat.

4 Block the scene in relation to the **axes** you have created in your design. Your throne doesn't need to be upstage centre; the blocking will change dramatically if you shift it onto a diagonal or place it laterally. You can lay a carpet runner or length of marking tape to represent an axis.

5 Be aware of the position of the scene in relation to the **rhythm** of the play. If a scene takes place in a section that moves quickly, opt for a simple blocking, particularly if the scene involves few characters. A meets B, they exit.

6   Try to define the **energy of a scene**. What is its pulse, its thrust? When Abraham enters in the rumble and the violence begins, the dynamic changes completely. It becomes driven. So what is the energy of the opening section? Are they lounging around in the midday sun, one blocking, or pacing up and down, hungry for a fight, a different blocking. Both will work. Get your actors to demonstrate both. A bold change of pace will help keep the story vivid and blocking will help this.

7   I sometimes make a distinction between **blocking** and **staging**. Blocking is the storytelling craft that propels the narrative and reveals your production. Staging is all of that plus the need to animate and choreograph the whole stage, which may be very large or just a tiny studio space. A classic example of a scene that requires real staging skills is the 'Sonnet' scene when Romeo first falls for Juliet at the Capulet ball. You will probably have the full company onstage for the party but you want the audience to focus on the lovers at this point. You can counterpoint them, by light or different movement qualities, the lovers still, the others slowly dancing around them; or maybe create a great sweeping staging that involves the whole company dancing, whirling, whirling around anti-clockwise and then suddenly … the stage is empty bar the two lovers. Here we have a staging that creates the desired effect of focusing the lovers, but additionally we communicate the special moment of falling in love when the whole world disappears, dissolves from consciousness and you only have eyes and ears for your lover.

8   Work on one section of a scene at a time: 1A, then 1B, then 1C, etc.

Blocking Large-scale Scenes

As a young director, I always dreaded scenes with many actors and complex plots within plots. Restoration comedy is particularly tricky and I directed a spectacularly bad production of Congreve's *Love for Love* at the Bristol Old Vic. This character had to talk to that character at one moment and then another a few lines later who had ended up right across the other side of the stage. A nightmare.

Shakespeare is much more friendly towards young directors. This is because there is often a key character to whom the rest of the cast refer: Duke Theseus in the opening scene of the *Dream*, King Claudius in the first court scene of *Hamlet*. If you endow such a character with status and power, much of the blocking will solve itself. Similarly, ask yourself who is the centre of attention of a scene? This may well shift from person to person, from Theseus to Egeus to Hermia. Stage energy will naturally revolve around each of those character in turn. Who is the centre of attention in the first Mechanical's scene, Bottom or Quince? Well, high status lies with Quince who is the director or convenor of the group, so give him a good position on the stage, possibly a chair, but the *power* lies with Bottom. The fun of the situation lies in the tension between status and power.

Occasionally Shakespeare will present you with a Restoration comedy challenge. The party scene in *Much Ado About Nothing* is an example; a series of encounters at a masked ball, coupled together by a dance. When faced with such a challenge, I would certainly broach the scene using my experimental 'tank', which would free up my actors and give my choreographer good material to work with.

Much of the detailed work of your middle section of rehearsal will revolve around defining and sharpening the **actions** of characters.

Refer back to our Awayday on Stanislavski. As the blocking develops, as the actors gain confidence in the scene on its feet, keep challenging your actors to define and sharpen their actions. 'What are you doing?' not 'What are you saying?' Point out the tools Shakespeare offers them in the language to achieve their wants. Encourage your actors to be vivid in their choices and rigorous with themselves. Banish the word 'persuade', it's obvious and generalized. This is one of the most exciting aspects of the director's role and it's true for any productions of any play, ancient or modern. *The uncovering, the discovery of the action of a character, can reveal the very soul of a human being and your job is to enable and nurture that revelation.*

As the middle section of rehearsals progresses, your actors will increasingly know more about the character's inner life than you do, and you must respect this. Their choice of actions will develop and change in the very heat of rehearsal. **It's as if they are possessed by the character.** I regard this as healthy and essential to the art of great acting. Some directors get rather fanatical about actioning and will argue: 'But I thought we agreed you would frighten him on that line and there you were cajoling him!' I don't hold with this as it inhibits an actor's imagination.

The chemistry of scene work lies in the interaction of one character's action and objective with those of another. A clash occurs, a conflict, which you must encourage and direct. However, conflict is not an end in itself; it is a byproduct of the clash of actions. An action or objective will have an **obstacle**, which is likely to be the actions and objectives of another character. This is called an **outer obstacle**. Take an obvious example, *A Midsummer Night's Dream,* Act 3 Scene 2. After Puck's mischievous work, Lysander loves Helena and Demetrius loves Helena. They each want to win her love. Clash, conflict. The obstacle here is twofold: each potential lover has a rival who loves her with equal passion, and Helena, the object of their love, is understandably reluctant to get emotionally hurt. They each must try a multitude of *activities* to make her choose them.

Some obstacles are internal to the character. 'I fancy that girl or boy, but am frightened of being rejected or am shy.' So your action in a scene will be tempered and shaped by your **inner obstacle**. In many ways, our characters are revealed more by our inner obstacle than our outer actions, as they reveal our vulnerabilities, likes and dislikes. So keep relating actions and obstacles to a developing character biography. For example, what is the source of Mercutio's cynicism about romantic love?

A typical fault of many actors, professional and amateur is to play the obstacle and not the action. The solution is to play the action stronger and to identify a more potent objective. You may need to remind the whole company of the world in which the play takes place. For example, in *Henry V*, the whole nation is at a crossroads and the bulk of the action takes place in a time of war. Encourage your actors to embrace the scale of the challenge – it is truly a matter of life or death.

Second Pass at Scenes

You have made a first pass at all the scenes. You have created a first blocking, which you should regard as provisional and flexible. You have begun the work on actioning and motivating. It's important that this work emanates from Shakespeare's language, or Pinter's, or Sarah Kane's, whoever is your author. Keep mining the language and adjust your choices accordingly.

As middle rehearsals progress, encourage your actors to get 'off the book' as soon as possible, in other words learn their lines and rehearse without carrying their scripts in their hands. The benefits are enormous. The very act of line learning requires the actor to become familiar with the thought processes of the character; rehearsing without scripts in hand allows an actor to fully engage with their partners in a scene and to **listen**! When the actor listens he/she can react; they are no longer in separate bubbles but in the same real time, the same space. All sorts of adjustments, major and minor will follow. Some actors delay learning their lines until the moves are set. This is understandable as the move and the thought become mutually suggestible. But it's rather selfish if your other actors are 'off the book' because it slows down the process and alters the nature of the rehearsal. When I return to scenes for a second time, I ask my stage management to write on the call the day before: 'Off the books for this scene please'. Alternatively announce through the daily call sheet or in person that you want books down by week two or week three.

Before you embark on a second pass, take a moment to reflect on the work so far. You will certainly find that some scenes are more advanced than others. That some scenes simply won't budge. That some scenes seem to have solved themselves. There's no rule that says you have to give each scene the same amount of time. Adjust your calls accordingly. Be aware that as rehearsals progress, some calls, like fights and choreography, will require a lot of time. Such calls will also need access to the main rehearsal space. So consider secondary calls. Can you take away one or two principals and do detailed work elsewhere? In a corridor perhaps? Or do you need to be present at all the fight/dance calls?

When I return to a scene for the second (or third) time, I ask the actors to go through the lines without moves, but *standing up*. This allows the actors to place the scene at the front of their thinking and allows you to sum up where you think you scene has arrived at. 'The stakes are not high enough.' 'The relationships are imprecise.' 'The scene feels static at this point in the story when we should be motoring.' Then let the scene run. They will probably have forgotten some of the blocking you worked on last time. This doesn't matter. Your DSM will have written down the moves and the actors (or you) might want to be reminded. Or you can adjust whatever moves your actors may have remembered. Or you might want to start again with new moves. You will find that progress is much quicker second time round and your actors can absorb masses more ideas and take on more complex challenges.

More important than the blocking is the quality of the actions, the interactions and the use of the language, and this is where most of your focus should be. It's the same agenda as earlier in the process: actions, activities and objectives made manifest through language. You will find that notes about 'how he does it', apposition, line endings, etc. will land much more potently second time round. As you develop your technique as a director, you may find that you are holding back many of these language connections to the second or third pass at scenes. You might see your first pass as a 'rough cut'. You need to judge how much detail an actor can absorb when he/she first tackles a scene. This will vary, actor to actor and scene to scene.

It's important to keep *challenging* the actor at this stage. There is a temptation to 'head for home', in other words simply try to improve the work you have already created. This is quite understandable. Your actors will have a whole raft of technical issues that need sorting. Help them if you can; it may be a simple matter of suggesting where in a speech they might breathe, or take a pause, or order the coffee from the waiter in the opening scene of *Romeo and Juliet*. But at the same time, try to open up the landscape of every scene you revisit. You may have got stuck on a scene or it may feel stale or you may simply not know what to with it. Your actors may not be 'firing' or are inhibited. They may feel **'blocked'**.

What to Do if Your Actors Get Inhibited or Stuck

Here are one or two things you might do.

- Ask the actors to run around the room two or three times as fast (and safely) as possible. Then run into the space and *immediately* play the scene, forgetting about blocking and verse and concept.
- Ask the actors to run to the end of an imaginary jetty at the ocean and shout out 'I want …' as wildly and loudly as possible, then run back and start the scene as above.
- In a two hander, ask the actors to stand against the walls as far away from each other as possible and play the scene. Encourage them to maintain as much detail as possible, in other words, don't just shout at each other.
- Ask the actors to play the scene as clearly and as seriously as possible, using the structure of the original, but talking gibberish or a made-up language. This will reveal how well they understand the shape of a scene.
- A variation on the above would be to use Shakespeare's language, only sung.
- In certain circumstances, you can rehearse a scene outside of the normal room. I rehearsed the Fool/Lear scenes in the

open air on Dover's Hill near Stratford. You could try Romeo meeting Juliet in a Starbucks.

The above exercises are designed to *throw the actor off-centre*. By this I mean to precipitate the actor into a less familiar, lesser-known territory. In this zone, he/she will react more instinctively, less rationally and will enter a more open, creative space. His/her subconscious will take over and, very often, important discoveries are made about a scene or a character.

I have sometimes used **animal exercises** to release a scene. This can have startling results. There are two forms of animal exercises both of which involve the selection of an animal and the impersonation of that animal in as visceral way as possible. Some research on the web will certainly be helpful. How does the animal move? Importantly, what is its centre of gravity? You should encourage your actors to become *possessed* by the animal. These exercises will only work if your actors are 'off the book'.

The purpose of the **first is to throw the actor off his or her centre**. You are best to start with a simple physical warm up or some non-verbal exercises. You would then select an animal as far away as possible from the actor's usual 'centre'. So for example, an actor might naturally be very shy, self-contained, organized, neat and tidy. You might select an animal far away from this. A predatory animal for example. A dangerous animal. Another actor might be self-confident and extravert. Choose an animal that has none of those characteristics. You would then put each actor involved in a particular scene, in a separate, imaginary 'cage', *as their animal*. You can use a few chairs for this if you wish. No talking allowed. They might start with the animal resting or sleeping and gradually awaken. Allow them time to explore their new physical being and their surroundings. You can provoke reaction by making a sudden noise or throwing items into the cage, a soft toy, a rolled up newspaper perhaps. The actors must remain in their cages and not share space with the other actors involved in the exercise. You will sense the actors becoming more and more involved with their animals. Then, without talking and with no discussion, get the actors to stand up and play the scene. If the exercise has done its magic, the actors will, unconsciously, have been thrown off their centre and discover new aspects to their character and the scene. Build on this work straight away. Give the actors feedback and go back over the scene incorporating ideas that have been thrown up.

The purpose of the **second** animal exercise is to **throw the actor towards the centre of the character**. You might be tackling the scene between Tybalt and Mercutio that leads to their deaths. Tybalt is described as 'fiery'. You would choose an animal that is proud, dangerous and unpredictable. Mercutio is mercurial, restless and also proud. Choose a suitable creature. The process would be the same as above, starting in separate cages. As the impro heats up, choose a moment to say 'Both in the same cage'. The animals will relate, circle each other, a danger will build up. Whatever you do, do not allow the exercise to become violent. If you see this is about to happen, *immediately* instruct the actors to play the scene, using Shakespeare's language. They may use your moves; they may not. The purpose of the exercise is to unlock the scene and bring a fresh, visceral element to the work.

Garments and props can sometimes 'unlock' a tricky scene or relationship and can lead to important discoveries that end up in the production. When Tony Sher played the Fool for me in *King Lear*, I wanted him to create a professional fool with real skills that he used in the production. One evening I brought in a tattered old bowler hat and a red ping-pong ball on a piece of elastic as a red nose. The character of the Fool was transformed. Tony created a Grock like creature, full of spite and wisdom and half-remembered music hall tricks. The hat and the nose released a floodgate of creativity which remained in the production, much in its original form.

By this time, you will have made a first and second pass at all of the scenes. You know there is still plenty to do and some scenes may seem intractable. Very often, an appreciation of the architecture of the whole play will solve problems in individual scenes. You are approaching the end of the second week of rehearsal, or the third if you have a longer period. So take the decision. Move on to the final movement.

15

Rehearsing the Play: End

This is the learning, revisiting and consolidating time.

Try to achieve **three run throughs.** It's important that you give yourself a couple of working days after the first run through to learn the lessons, revisit as much of the play as possible and rebalance the production. Therefore aim for one at the end of the penultimate week or the beginning of the final week, one towards the end of your last week and one on your final day of rehearsals. In other words: Friday (penultimate week), Wednesday and the final Friday. Or, Monday, Thursday and the final Friday.

You will find that you learn volumes from your **first run through**, which is why you need a clear two days to rework. Involve your actors. They will know immediately what does and doesn't feel right. They might not have the solutions straightaway and they will look to you for help and guidance. Encourage them to share their thoughts and be clear and honest with them in return. It's not a bad idea to invite them to criticize their own work. But you have to be confident to do this and trust their judgement.

Be prepared to change course. There's a philosophical but practical point here. Is the goal of rehearsals to arrive at the perfect manifestation of your imagined production? Or to make a journey with your cast and arrive at a destination which might be unexpected but none the less wonderful. I try to attempt the latter, but am much tempted by the former. The production of a play is an organic, evolving, growing process. You might not end up exactly where you anticipated, but don't be afraid to embrace change. Remember: 'Feel passion for everything, but cling to nothing.' So don't be afraid to chuck things out. Run throughs and previews are the proper times to embrace change. I once re-blocked most of the final act of *Dr Faustus* in Manchester on the Press Night. If Ben Kingsley was thrown by this, he certainly didn't show it. The performance was faultless.

So, what are you looking out for in your first run through?

Is the story clear? If not, why not?
Is it slow?
How about the performances? Are they on the right lines? Is someone getting left behind or acting in a different production?
Can you understand the language? Can you hear everybody?
Is the blocking clear, 'readable'?
Is your production clear, readable?
Does your production make sense?!

First run through: How does it work?

Firstly, give your company and stage management at least two days' notice of a first run. Maybe have a quiet word with the leading actor if he/she has a huge part. The actors will want to pace themselves and the stage management will want to make sure all props are set in the right place and they have a plan for quick changes of scene.

Be aware that a first run through is a very scary time for every actor. They need your support.

Before the run, gather the company together. Perhaps do a quick, brisk warm up. Remind them of why the play is important, talk about the stage you are at in rehearsals, talk about what you want to achieve, what they should focus on. On a first run through, don't ask for award-winning performances. I often advise the actors to take a measured approach. Tell the story clearly. Focus on getting the blocking right. Focus on good clear communications with your fellow actors. Don't set the oven too high. Or I might set a specific task, for example I might ask the actors in *Henry V* to think about who they have left behind in England. If you need a prompt, ask for one clearly. Warn them that you will be taking notes. Any questions? Does the stage manager need to say anything?

For the first run through, you might consider a more *staggered approach*. I learnt this when I was assistant to Ron Daniels at RSC.

You run the first scene. You stop, you give very fast notes, general and specific. Just a couple of minute's worth.

You re-run the first scene and follow right on and run the second scene. You stop and give notes on the second scene.

You re-run the second scene and follow into the third scene. Stop, note it and continue in this way through the play.

It's a fascinating exercise. You will find that the work improves *immeasurably* between the first and second passes at a scene. You will also find that an energy builds up and the company want to be let loose like greyhounds. So if I opt for this method of running, I will follow this pattern for the first three or four scenes and then let the run through just take its course.

You will take a break at the interval. Don't go and hide. Wander the room and be available and supportive.

Take notes as you go along. Try not to be too intrusive! I write specific notes at the front of my notebook and general notes at the back. That way, I can better order my thoughts for the note session. As you watch, you will probably get new ideas, a better way of staging this scene, a different entrance for that character. Scribble all these thoughts down at the back of your book.

How to Give Your Notes

After the first run, take a fifteen-minute break, find somewhere quiet and get your thoughts straight. Your impressions and general feelings are important. Gather the company and **give your notes**. Thank them and point out that you quite appreciate the challenges of a first run through, remembering the lines, scenes arriving thick and fast, being ambushed by the speed the events unfolded. Your notes might follow this pattern:

1. Start with general notes. Long shot rather than close-up, to use a cinematic metaphor. Does the production have dramatic energy? Does the production have a strong forward motion, like an inner hunger? Are the stakes sufficiently high? If the answer to any of these questions is 'No' or 'Not sure', then you can be certain that the wants and objectives are insufficiently strong. This analysis will give a context to more specific notes.

You might think parts of the play were slow. Be specific: Where was it slow? Why was it slow? Obviously, unfamiliarity with lines will be part of the problem but almost certainly it will be because actions weren't being played sufficiently strongly. What about the overall shape? Perhaps it didn't feel sufficiently dramatic? What's at stake? Is it life or death? Remind them of the world as researched and discovered in rehearsal. But don't just be negative. What are the *positive* impressions and achievements. What was great, what elements were vivid and exciting. Try to identify the *cause* and not just the *effect* of an impression you had. For example, you might think the Mechanicals in the *Dream* were warm and funny. Why? Tell them it was because of the accuracy of the world they created and the detail in the scenes.

2. Give general notes about the quality of the language work. A lot of detail may well have got lost. Remind them that skillful use of Shakespeare's language will empower them and give specificity to character work. Give some examples from the run through. After the first 'stagger through' of his production of *Hamlet* at Stratford, John Barton went right back to basics. He sat the cast down for two whole days and went through the play, line by line. He had the time, but, crucially, it was a *priority*.

3. Give notes about performances and character, always identifying the root of problems and not just the impression.

4. Go through the play scene by scene. Don't be too finicky. A lot of detail will be recovered when you rework through the play.

5. Conclude. Set the agenda for the next period of rehearsals. You will rework the whole play quickly, scene by scene and

then do a second run through. What do you want them to focus on? Have they learnt the text accurately?

Use the weekend to go over your thoughts and prepare for the final week. Are the big movements of the play clear? Is the rhythm right? Is the world alive and logical? What are the weak performances? How can you help? Are the relationships accurate? Are the cuts working? Do you need any more cuts? If so, this is the perfect time to implement them.

This is an exciting moment in rehearsal but also a moment of decision. There may be flaws in your original concept and these will start to reveal themselves as the days pass. Be honest with yourself. Have you communicated your ideas clearly or are there fundamental cracks? A rehearsal process takes on a life of its own and, as we've noted many times, the journey may take an unexpected direction. You must decide to adapt and evolve or make your original thoughts more robust and vivid.

During this time, stay close to your leading actors. Find time for one-on-one conversations. There will be urgent matters, great and small, and they will want time to talk through their experiences and ideas.

Second and Third Run Throughs

Now work through the whole play at a faster tempo. This is a period of rehearsal when you really must control the room. There might not be much time for lengthy discussion. Demand a maximum concentration. Be quite honest with your cast. Some actors will simply not know it well enough. An actor who is dodgy on lines will not only be holding him/herself back, but the other actors also. If I'm getting a rotten cue, how can I deliver my lines and thoughts accurately? Tell the culprit to sharpen up. In rehearsal, knowledge does not grow at a steady, constant pace; the process speeds up exponentially the closer you get to opening. You can work faster and your actors will absorb information and make adaptations quicker, defter and with more assurance. They will improve their performances enormously between run throughs even if you say absolutely nothing. Like a coach in sport, you are aiming at 'match fitness'. You might try 'mini runs'. You may have revisited four or five scenes in an afternoon. Use the final thirty minutes to run that section. No need to pre-announce. Just do it.

The **second and third run throughs** should be closer together.

You can prepare your cast for their first audience in the rehearsal room. First of all, don't get stuck in one position at the front. Move your chair to the side of the action or just stand to one side. Your actors will unconsciously start to open out their performances. I shadowed Jean-Louis Barrault in Paris; he directed much of the show *Harold et Maude* from the wings. If you are running a scene, get the actors who are not in that particular scene to watch from all around and encourage the actors in the scene to *share* the action and the language with the whole room, 360 degrees. The great director and activist Joan Littlewood would frequently shout out at her actors while they were rehearsing (I can imagine her calling 'That's boring!' or 'I don't believe a word!'). There was never any danger of her actors being ambushed by the arrival of the audience.

You should invite your creative team and technical staff to one of the later run throughs. It's important for them to see the work in progress to fulfil their tasks. Be aware that sometimes the techies aren't the most vocal of audiences. You might find that a scene that has elicited gales of laughter in rehearsal is met by a stony silence. But this won't be the silence of judgement; it will be the silence of concentration. They are doing their jobs and working through the technical consequences of the work you have been doing.

Set aside quality time after rehearsal to go through the production with your creative associates. You will have talked through your ideas for light, sound and music before rehearsals began and, hopefully, your collaborators will have popped into rehearsal to get a sense of progress and maybe try out one or two ideas on you. If it's possible to try out some music or sound cues in a run through, all well and good, but make sure you pre-warn the cast.

I always seek feedback from my closest creative partners. It can get very lonely in the later days of rehearsals. This will help you set *priorities*. After the second run through, you might only have a single session before the final run through. What will you concentrate on? The detail of a scene will very often take care of itself if the shape and action is right. You must recognize that the dynamics of rehearsal have changed now you are running. Consider this metaphor: the scenes of a play are individual jewels, some small, bright, perfect, some large and vulgar. String them together into a necklace and they create a different object. You, as director, must now judge the whole necklace as well as the individual jewels.

Take time in your notes to describe to the cast how the show is developing. Articulate what it's like to watch the show. Share the discoveries you are making. When I started running *Macbeth* in Stratford, I realized that the series of scenes that follow the assassination of Duncan have a pattern that closely resembles the events that follow the inception of tyranny in many modern states. I described these scenes as 'Fears and Miseries', taking my cue from

Brecht's sequence of short plays. The terror starts close to the centre of power, then seeps out across the country and then into neighbouring England. This enabled us to reconceptualize a part of the play that can often seem anti-climactic.

Your cast will also be developing at different rates. You may find your Mechanicals in the *Dream* are way ahead of the rest of the cast and only need an audience. Keep suggesting small challenges. You may need to pull back the comic exuberance of some of your cast. My revival of *The Duchess of Malfi* in Paris was badly marred by the fact that I failed to spot the Cardinal veering off in a different direction to the rest of the cast. When I realized what was happening (during previews) it was too late. The laughter he elicited bred laughter in adjacent, more serious scenes.

It is also important to balance the different elements in a comedy. Laughter, although important, is not the only valid currency. In the *Dream*, pathos, emotional engagement and drama are also important. In *Romeo and Juliet*, humour plays an important part. In *Henry V*, there is the vital emotional release of the Katherine scenes and the eccentricity of Fluellen.

Preparing for the Theatre

On your final day, you will say goodbye to the rehearsal room and prepare for the technical rehearsal and previews, if you are lucky enough to have them.

These are some of the things I might say to my cast:

- I will thank them for their work and their company.

- I will try to recap the *story of the rehearsal process*. How the work developed, the highs, the lows, the important discoveries.
- I will point out how much their performances have developed over the last few days.
- I will give them one or two tasks to think over during the tech rehearsal.
- I will warn them that they may lose touch with the play during the tech. What with costumes, lighting, sound effects and music, it's easy to feel alienated. This will pass as they begin to own the stage, and ingest the other elements into their performances.
- I will remind them that it is a *technical* rehearsal and my focus will not always be on the actors. They will certainly have to repeat things many times for the benefit of the technical crew.
- I'll tell them not to waste energy, especially vocal energy. The sound crew will need to hear full volume at least once to set levels, but don't act full on for hours. You'll shred your voice.
- I'll invite the stage manager to talk through the schedule and make any necessary 'housekeeping' remarks.

And if I've got time, I'll ask everyone for a drink!

16

Tech, Dress, Previews and Opening

The 'Tech'

It's the morning of the 'tech'. You arrive at the stage door and introduce yourself to the stage doorkeeper who points you towards the stage. You negotiate unfamiliar corridors, fading posters of old shows, fire extinguishers and health and safety notices. Stairways in unexpected places. Doors to the left and right. A member of the wardrobe department bats past you carrying an armful of costumes. You recognize one or two of the fabrics. Good morning! Through that door at the end, another corridor and you're there! The stage. It's dark and you hear the voice of your lighting designer calling to an unseen colleague. They're focusing lanterns one by one. You walk out into the space and peer into the darkened auditorium, lit only by a row of computer screens and a couple of anglepoise lamps. Breathe deeply. It's your show!

I freely admit, I find a theatre during a tech period one of the most exciting places on earth. To this day, I can shut my eyes and summon the particular smell of backstage at the Bristol Old Vic, where I started my career. Ditto the Royal Shakespeare Theatre in Stratford, now demolished. In that darkened space, you create a whole world, you tell a story by carving with light, surrounding the audience with sound and music and by serving, supporting and framing your actors. Above, I describe arriving at one of the dozens of proscenium theatres that exist across the UK, but the same thrill and sense of infinite possibility exists if you're working in a small studio, a room over a pub or a university theatre, amateur or professional.

How to Set Up a Tech

There are two purposes of a tech rehearsal:

1 To place the production as rehearsed into the space.
2 To integrate the 'technical' elements of light, video, sound and music with your staging.

There are other secondary but important factors you need to bear in mind:

- You must ensure that all technical departments have enough information and time to do their jobs. Remember, it is a *technical* rehearsal, so don't spend ages discussing a change of motivation with your actors- it's simply not fair on everyone else.
- Don't try to do everyone else's job. Assume they have expertise. Final decisions are, of course, yours.
- Help the stage management organize the time and try to keep to the schedule. The amount of time allotted for a tech rehearsal is invariably tight for logistical and financial reasons. In the commercial theatre it might be very costly having a full

staff but no box office income. At the Edinburgh Fringe you may need to tech in just a couple of hours as another show will be sharing the space and following you in.
- Be prepared to make adjustments as necessary. You will see your work with fresh eyes and may need to make changes. Some changes are best made later; some require an instant remedy. For example, you might realize that you have placed one of Henry's monologues far too far upstage; you will need to adjust this straight away so the lighting designer can make the necessary adjustments. Modern lighting boards are fast and changes can be made and recorded very quickly.
- Try to help the actors 'own' the space. Moving into the theatre can be very disorientating and, as explained, can engender a sense that they are losing the play. It's important that they feel comfortable in the *costumes*. There may be changes and adjustments that need to happen. In consultation with your designer, give a steer on what *make-up* is required. The days of heavy lines and '5 and 9' have long passed, but eye make-up is often very helpful under stage lights. Encourage your actors to use the tech time wisely and *practise* with the set. If they have costume changes, plan these meticulously.
- It's *vital* that the DSM creates a clear well-organized 'book'. In many respects this is the bible of your show. It's usually set out as follows: the script is printed on the right hand side of a folder or binder and on the left side, on a blank sheet, is written all the moves that have been created in rehearsal and clear lines drawn across the page connecting to lighting, sound, music and video cues at specific points in the text. This enables the DSM to coordinate the contributions of the different departments, so, for example, lights, music and video all start at *exactly* the same moment. It enables the director

to make adjustments to his/her effects in a precise way. You may say 'I want the lighting effect to go three words before the music starts.' The DSM will adjust the book. And should the DSM fall ill, a colleague could take over instantly.

So, **how do you run a tech?**

Firstly, agree with your stage manager (SM) how you want to work. He/she will probably be very experienced at organizing a tech and will be a great ally. In an ideal situation, the SM will be on the stage, the DSM will be in the auditorium near the director and the ASM will be in the wings helping the actors with entrances, props, etc.

Start the day with the whole company, cast, technical crew, wardrobe, everybody assembled onstage. Welcome everybody, make introductions if necessary and talk briefly about the show and how you hope the rehearsal will proceed. Ask your actors not to leave the stage area until they have been cleared by the SM. Ask them to work clearly and accurately. The DSM needs precise cues. At this point, the SM must talk about **safety** issues. Theatres can be extremely dangerous places. There will likely be a requirement to walk from light into dark and dark into light. Use the tech time to practise these in the correct lighting state. In many plays, weapons are used. Strictly forbid any mucking about and ensure that fight rehearsals are only held under supervision.

Preferably, you will start at the top of the play. Occasionally, with a complex set, the SM and technical crew will ask for a set-change rehearsal before the actors come onstage. This can save a lot of time and grief. In opera, it is usual for costumes to be held back until the Dress Rehearsal; I much prefer to tech in costume for most of the time as it allows the cast to inhabit the costumes. Costumes become clothes.

So, start at the very beginning. Remember, *everything* must go in the book. If there is pre-show music, play it; the DSM will record the moment it begins and ends in the book. Rehearse the start of the show in detail. Imagine as precisely as possible how you want it to look and sound. Here's how the opening of *Romeo and Juliet* might start in our 'choral' version.

The house lights are on, there is a lighting 'preset' on the stage and music is playing.

House lights dim to half (to allow members of the audience to sit down and shut up).

House lights and onstage preset fade to black.

SM cues on the full company from the wings in the darkness.

Lights fade up on the company onstage and simultaneously fade out the music.

And the company begins the speech. Stop. Check everyone feels safe and the detail of the cuing is in the book. Adjust and repeat. Do you like it? Can you improve it? If there are simple, quick fixes, do them now. Otherwise, make a note, check with the DSM and move on.

You will need to concentrate on the scene changes and allow good time to practise. Check with the SM that they are safe and as efficient as possible. What if you discover that a scene change is much longer than you anticipated? You may need to ask your composer or sound designer to contribute some more music or perhaps you might invent a short piece of narrative action with your actors to avoid stopping and starting.

Focus on the entrances and exits. Distances will be different in the theatre. My advice is to keep the links between scenes as tight as possible. You will find that this helps build up energy onstage. Scene 2 piggybacks on the energy of scene 1. I use an image to actors: imagine the stage is a hot plate; it is your responsibility to keep it hot so the play cooks!

Work your way through the play. There will be times when you only have time to sketch in an effect. It is preferable to plot something in the lighting computer to improve later than spend hours finessing a complex sequence. Watch people's energy levels. Ensure others take proper breaks and mind you do too.

You will arrive at the end with 1,001 things still to do, but the clock is ticking and you will need to move on.

The 'Dress'

This should be what it says it is, a dress *rehearsal*. It's a time for everyone, cast and crew alike, to practise, improve and plot. If you are lucky enough to have the time for more than one Dress Rehearsal, use the first one as a technical run through. Paradoxically, by focusing on the technical aspects, it takes the pressure off the actors to perform. And they will certainly have enough technical concerns to deal with: new props, costume changes, negotiating a darkened backstage, make-up (if you have decided to use any). So I will tell the actors in advance to focus their energies on the *mechanics* of the production; the heart and soul of their performances will follow.

It is helpful to have a *warm up* onstage, a good hour or hour and a half before curtain up. It allows the company to re-form as a unit, to test the acoustics and prepare as a group. Ideally this should be repeated before all subsequent performances. Run the Dress Rehearsal as closely as possible to show conditions. The rehearsal should be run by the SM and called as per show, with the 'Half Hour' called (in fact 35 minutes before curtain up), the 'Five' (10 minutes before show) and 'Beginners' (5 minutes before).

You may want to invite one or two friends or colleagues to watch and provide helpful feedback. A full, invited audience is a pretty scary option and I rarely go down that route, but occasionally it can be just what the show needs to lift it to a new level. Ron Field, my American choreographer on *Kiss Me Kate*, asked for such a run, quite common on Broadway, and it lifted the show like a shot of adrenaline.

You should allow your tech team to carry on working through the Dress. This means adjusting the light levels and tweaking the sound. They will be very discrete. Forewarn the actors that this work will continue. Take detailed technical notes; this is your best opportunity to get adjustments into the 'book'. If the book is not precise, the show will never be precise.

As the show unfolds, in between the mass of technical information you are processing, you will gain some very strong, very useful impressions of your production. Write these down at the back of your notebook and *hang onto them*. They are invaluable. They may be quite simple; it's too dark, it's too slow. They may be more complex and need careful thought. For example you might think that this or that performance is not real. Or you might think that the subplot is not balanced with the main dramatic thrust. Or that you have created too many endings (the *Dream* seems to have several written into the text!). Think quickly. Many of these issues can be addressed through notes and the sooner the company address them, the better.

So straight after the run, gather the company onstage and make general observations. Almost certainly you will want to address the subject of *audibility*. It's only natural, moving from a rehearsal room to a stage, that audibility will suffer. Audibility is partly a function of technique and practice but also of strong actioning and working the language. Remind them of the work done in rehearsal: play strong actions, play the antitheses, relish the rhymes, don't drop the ends of your lines or run over the verse like prose. Most actors find it very useful if you tell it straight. This bit is too slow. There's not enough at stake in that scene. After a Dress run of *Mephisto* at the Barbican, I told the actors, reluctantly, that it was boring. Surprisingly, Alan Rickman, playing one of the leads, turned to his fellow actors and said 'That's great! That's useful. It's boring and we must all do something about it.' And together we did.

If you have time, give quick notes on individual scenes and performances, bearing in mind you have asked them to focus on technical matters! Remember, at this stage in the process, a cast can take onboard many revisions that would take hours earlier on. If you run out of time, go round the dressing rooms with individual notes. There will certainly be backstage matters that might need your attention although most of these should be dealt with by the SM.

Allow as much time as possible after the run for technical notes. Gather the full tech crew. Thank them for getting you to this point. If there are general notes give them first (e.g. the first scene in Romeo feels like night time and I want it to feel like Noon in Naples). Then go through the play, scene by scene, as quickly and efficiently as possible. Be precise and ensure that you have communicated to the DSM exactly what you want. Hear what problems or confusions exist and deal with them.

At this stage of rehearsal, time will always be at a premium whether you are directing a university show, a fringe show or a Shakespeare at the National Theatre. If you are at the National, there will be time for a second Dress Rehearsal at which you will be able to focus much more on the performances and the shape and tone of the production. The above scenario of Tech and Dress Rehearsal will pertain whatever your circumstances. Wherever you are directing there will always be one or two people, 'stakeholders', who will want to contribute. This might be the director of the theatre, the producer or the president of the uni dramatic society. You need to be tactful but careful. Such people can easily knock your self-confidence. Indeed, this is exactly what happened to me at university. Over the years, on balance, I have found such input helpful. But finally, it is *your* production and it will be judged as such. Own it, flaws and all.

Curtain Calls

I *hate* staging **curtain calls**.

But it has to be done and is best done straight after one of the Dress Rehearsals. It's an important part of the audience's experience and should be well organized, disciplined and appropriate to your production. It's a way of saying 'thank you' to the audience. Plan the call in advance and write it down. Stage it quickly and efficiently and leave time to practise a couple of times. This will allow the lighting crew to create states and the stage management to record cues. I avoid discussion and debate. If you don't like what you've staged, you can change it later.

With a Shakespeare play, I will base my call around company bows. I will bring on the whole company and ask them to make one or two bows ensemble. I will then have some of the principal actors walk forward from the group and take separate calls, sometimes in pairs, sometimes solus. I will then clear the stage completely. In certain circumstances, I will bring back one or two of the actors who have carried most of the burden. King Lear, obviously, Romeo and Juliet, separately or, perhaps, coming on from opposite sides of the stage and meeting. The principal actors might then be joined by the whole group for one or two more company bows.

The old-fashioned way was to start with the small part players, then the supporting actors and then the leads. Known in the trade as a 'Who's Best'. This has the advantage of building the applause to a climax. You will still see this in opera and the West End. At the other extreme, you might see a curtain call in which those with huge parts get no individual calls. This seems unfair on the audience and on the actors who have taken on major roles. It's also dishonest, because responsibility and talent are not equally distributed in theatre. I go for a middle way. You might choose some music to accompany the bows. Think of your curtain call as a short narrative, with a beginning, middle and end. The climax should be a shared moment between cast and audience.

Previews

When I began my professional career at the Bristol Old Vic, the Dress took place in the afternoon and we opened to a paying public and the critics the same evening. The same applied when I directed students at RADA. Not until I worked at the Manchester Royal Exchange and the RSC did I enjoy the luxury of a **Preview**.

Previews are much more common now right across the theatre, national companies, fringe, regional and sometimes student productions. The reason is simple; it can improve the work immeasurably. When your production encounters an audience for the first time you will see your work in a fresh light. Rather, it's *possible* to see your work in a fresh light, if you have ears to hear and eyes to see. Experienced actors will likewise look forward to a first Preview as it will help them to advance their performance to the next level. An audience will have heard none of your ideas, digested none of your research; they will simply see and hear what is communicated. An audience will hunt out the main story, they will latch onto characters and situations and follow them. They might laugh at unexpected places. They might not laugh at all! An alchemy occurs when an audience congregates and it is vital for the director, who is amongst them, to sense this near magical process. Which is why, for the first Preview, I always sit smack in the middle of the house and hang about, anonymously, in the intermission. Try and sense what is happening. Don't be too downhearted if things don't unfold as you imagined. A Shakespeare play is not a sprint. It can take time for a play to weave its spell. I was told when I joined the RSC 'Oh, you get the first ten minutes for free; after that you have to win them.' Most important of all, an audience can teach you about your production, not just what works and what doesn't, but, more profoundly, the very *meaning* of a play.

Here's an example. I directed Jonathan Pryce in *Macbeth*. In rehearsal, we created an intense vortex of energy; characters came in and out of his field of concentration. He embarked on a journey of spiritual decadence which led, inevitably, to destruction. Jonathan kept his focus almost entirely inward, his eyes to the ground. In the rehearsal room, it was quite awesome. Onstage, I lit the show with two follow spots out front and two above the action like cat's eyes. We were quite certain we had created something quite special. Then, with the first Preview, nothing. The audience showed minimal interest. Horrible! Driving back to my digs, I realized what was going on. This amazing charisma that had been created simply wasn't communicating. The audience weren't included. They watched but were not drawn in. The solution was simple: the next night Jonathan engaged with the house throughout the play and used direct eye contact in his soliloquies. A transformation! We learnt that the experience has to be both public and private at one and the same time. As it would have been in Shakespeare's lifetime. It's always worth encouraging your actors to have direct eye contact with the audience during their soliloquies. Cinema is a private experience, a Shakespeare play is public.

Gather your cast after the Preview or Public Dress. You will be very short of time, so what's important? You must convey to the actors the *experience* of being in the audience. *This is much more important than telling them what they did wrong.* Describe the experience as vividly as you can, relating it to the goals and ambitions of your production. Identify where the audience followed the story and where they got lost. Suggest improvements. Tell them if there were problems of audibility. A telltale sign of this will be restlessness. In a fundamental way, a production *doesn't exist* until it encounters an audience, so try to sum up how your original vision is developing. For example, I originally thought that *Henry V* was a play about leadership; during previews, I realized it was about building a nation. This allowed me to *re-tell the story* to the actors laying special emphasis on Shakespeare's creation of a multilayered society that gels and gains identity during a time of conflict. This subtly rebalanced the show. I believe that this is the time to allow a production to breathe and to allow the actors more autonomy. The actor's job is no longer to 'get it right'. In many respects, ownership shifts from director to acting company. Encourage responsibility, give confidence and don't cling. Be honest, adult to adult. Some directors find this time extremely difficult. They become possessive, unwilling or unable to let go.

If you do have time for a **second Preview**, husband the time wisely. If there is a whole day before the next performance, consider allowing a bit of sleep-in time for the cast. Do your technical rework first and then just call one or two actors. Maybe have a sandwich lunch with your leading actor to talk through more detail. Perhaps there is a shift of emphasis you want to achieve. This happened on *Hamlet* with Branagh. I felt some of the amazing 'gear shifts' he had discovered in rehearsal had smoothed out.

Now decide how you want to use your last session. You could do another run through; this might be too tiring. Or specific scenes. Or perhaps **'speed run'** particular sections. This can be highly rewarding. You run a specified section of the play, including every line, every move, motivation and action. No props, just mime them. Get them to play as fast and accurately as possible. This is not just an exercise in tightening cues; it can galvanize and sharpen the whole experience. The lesson to learn here is think and speak at the same time, on the line, with the cue. Don't stop, think and then reply; think as you answer.

Opening

I invariably watch the opening night or Press Night of my productions. I don't take notes. I find it cathartic, a rite of passage. It liberates me. Occasionally I will have a Damascene revelation and realize I have missed an obvious opportunity. When he was working in London, John Dexter would give his final notes then catch the next plane back to New York and rarely see the production again. There are directors who watch every single performance of their productions, which many actors find oppressive. Some directors read every word written about the show in the newspapers and will even enter correspondence with the critics if the reviews are not glowing. Some directors never read a word. Most directors are disappointed if their reviews don't include the words wonderful, counsellor, mighty, everlasting. I do read reviews. It's often hard to swallow, but critics can sometimes have very valuable insight and analysis. This is especially true of critics who dedicate their lives to the art form.

If you are directing a show that has just three or four performances, perhaps in a student situation, watch every performance, but give a different brief for each show. This might be technical, for example with the *Dream* you might ask the actors to relish all the rhymes; or interpretive, for example, ask every actor in *Henry V* to imagine a burning, urgent reason why they might despise or be fearful of the French/English.

However short the run of performances, try to create a journey with the actors. Your production is an organic, developing entity that comes alive with an audience and changes. Like a child, you must let it grow up, let it go.

And so ... back to where we started. You.

Directing a Shakespeare play will change you for ever. You will have travelled a long distance, emotionally and intellectually. You will have learnt as much about yourself as about the play. You may have made lifelong friends. I hope that it sparks an appetite for the classics that will live with you always. To this day, I constantly refer back to the lessons I learnt in my training and my early days as a director, my 'formation' as the French perfectly describe it. However many productions I have directed, I always feel apprehensive and nervous about embarking upon the next. I invariably feel that I'm starting from scratch. I wonder how I could possibly have directed this or that play, not knowing what I now know. But I retain, deep inside me, the certainty that I looked at the mountain, approached it, respected it and then climbed it.

Good luck.

Index

actions 36–7, 118, 119–22, 173, 188–90, 192
actors
   auditions 113–15
   blocked 193–6
   building a character 158–61
   casting the actor or the part 111–13
   challenging during rehearsals 192
   company of 112, 115, 156–8
   costume design 101
   cuts to the text 127–8, 136–7
   discussing character during rehearsals 172–4
   dyslexic 152
   finishing speeches 67
   freelance status 109
   hinge moment 153
   improvisation 156
   journey of 30
   limited experience 110
   memory triggers 160–1
   micing 108
   mutual respect 3–4
   off the book 191
   possession by the character 189
   power of 4
   rehearsal garments 149, 159
   scale figures of 86–7
   technical rehearsal 205–6, 209
   throwing off centre 194
   throwing towards the centre 195
   value of preview 218
   vocational training 110
Alcina (Handel) 71–2
alliteration 59–61
analysis of play 26–30
ancient Geek theatre 14
Angels in America (Kushner) 16
animal exercises 194
Anthony and Cleopatra (Shakespeare) 148
apposition 24, 27, 46–50, 123–4
As You Like It (Shakespeare)
   emotions 118
   extreme actions 36–7
   female relationships 34
   forest metaphor 29
   paradigm of change 16
   skeleton of the play 83
assistant stage manager (ASM) 150, 210
assonance 59–61
atmos 94, 102
audibility issues 214
audience 26, 30, 106–7, 217–18
auditions 113–15
axes of the scene 80–1, 87, 90, 92, 186

Barrault, Jean-Louis 7, 97, 203
Barton, John 172, 201
battles 28, 29, 43, 64–5, 89, 121–2
Beerbohm, Max 150
beginning, middle and end
   speech structure 64–6
   summary story of play 25–6
Bernstein, Leonard 162
Berry, Cicely 107
biographies of characters 166, 173–4
Blake, Howard 105
blocked actors 193–6
blocking 140, 144–5, 182–90, 192
book creation by DSM 150, 209–10
brainstorming 73
Branagh, Kenneth 121, 219
Brand (Ibsen) 182
Bristol Old Vic 10, 69–70, 188, 216
Brook, Peter 90
Burbage, Richard 3, 128
Burgess, Anthony 63
Bush, Kate 88

calls 149, 175–6, 191, 213
Campbell, Cheryl 159
cast list 17–24, 32–4
casting the play 109–15
   auditions 113–15
   casting director 115
   casting the actor or the part
      111–13
   composing a company 112, 115
   recalls 114
Cathy Come Home (Loach) 16
chairs
   design process 89
   in rehearsals 157, 160, 179, 182, 185, 195
   on stage 86
change, director's role 16
Chekov, Anton

Cherry Orchard, The 160–1
Seagull 107
Cherry Orchard, The (Chekov)
   160–1
Chorus 15, 24, 54, 55, 176–7
Churchill, Winston 123
class groupings 34
Clockwork Orange, A (Burgess) 63
collaboration 70, 71, 111
colour 95–7
comedy 35, 49, 79, 136, 205
Comedy of Errors, The (Shakespeare)
   master and servant relationship
      166–7
   music 106–7
Commedia dell'arte 166
company of actors 112, 115, 156–8
confusion 27, 28, 30
costume
   design process 99, 100–1
   rehearsals 148–9, 159, 196, 209, 210–11
Cottrell, Richard 10
courtyard theatres 92
crisis 27, 30
critic reviews 219–20
Crowley, Bob 69, 85
curtain calls 215–16
cut away 48
cut every line bar one exercise 67
cuts 127–37
   actor's viewpoint 127–8, 136–7
   choice of edition 136–7
   length 129–30
   read through 152
   shape 130–7
   time line of play 130–6
   working out number of lines to be cut 129–30
   writer's viewpoint 128
cyclorama 82, 96

Daniels, Ron 199
Davy, Shaun 105, 107
decoration 95–7
deputy stage manager (DSM) 150, 209–10
design process
    analysis and discussion 72–3
    axes 80–1, 87, 90, 92
    brainstorming 73
    chair use 89
    colour 95–7
    concept 99
    costume design 99, 100–1
    decoration 95–7
    as a developing sculpture 84
    entrances and exits 78–80, 87–8, 90, 92
    floors 77–8, 87
    furniture use 92, 94–5
    getting stuck 99
    in the round 90–2
    journey of the play 84–6
    juxtaposition 49
    lighting design 49, 87, 88, 99, 101–2
    listening to criticism 98
    mechanics of the play 77–82
    methodology 75–84
    model stage 74–5
    music 103–8
    projection 88–9
    reading the play out loud 72
    relationship with designer 69–71
    scene changes 49, 94–5
    show and tell 97–8
    skeleton 83–4
    sound designer 107–8
    space of the play 75–6
    storyboards 97
    technology 94–5
    texture 95–7
    thrust stages 92–4
    wall of ideas 71–2
    walls 82–3
Dexter, John 128, 219
disorientation 29
Dogville (von Trier) 185
Doll's House, A (Ibsen) 90, 148, 159
Dr Faustus (Marlowe) 198
dramatic energy 24, 45–67
dress rehearsal 212–15
Duchess of Malfi (Webster) 205

emotions 9, 29, 118
empowerment 41
energy 35, 75, 80, 107, 182, 187, 217
    dramatic energy 24, 45–67
enhancement 108
entrances and exits 78–80, 87–8, 90, 92
epic story 35
ethnic diversity 111–12
experience, widening 11, 12
extreme actions 36–7

family groups 18, 20, 32–3
'feel' of the play 36
female roles 34, 111–12
Field, Ron 213
Fiennes, Ralph 182
fight scenes 146, 210
film directing 30
First Time rule 28
floors 77–8, 87
Forest, The (Ostrovsky) 3
forests
    design process 83, 87–8, 89
    as a metaphor 29
Foxworth, Bob 85
Friel, Brian 128
friendship groups 33
full stops 58–9, 124
furniture 92, 94–5, 148, 185–6

Gambon, Michael 85, 119, 148
'gates' 160–1
gender of cast 19, 34, 111–12
Globe Theatre 14–15, 61
group sculpture 162–3

Hamlet (Shakespeare)
   apposition 46–7
   changing landscapes 29
   metaphor 50–1
   previews 219
   run through 201–2
   tank exercise 179–81
Hands, Terry 172
Harold et Maude 203
headline 64–6
Henry V (Shakespeare)
   actions 119–21
   apposition 48–9, 123–4
   beginning, middle and end exercise 25
   blocking 185
   cast list 21–4, 32
   Chorus 15
   confusion 27
   crisis 27
   entrances and exits 79–80
   extreme actions 36
   family groups 32
   friendship groups 33
   iambic pentameter 53–4
   language 41–4, 171
   line endings 57–9, 124–5
   metre and pulse 124
   music 105
   previews 218
   resolution 28, 29
   rhythm 55
   status games 165
   storytelling 64–5
   structure 122–3

   vocabulary 125
   world of the play 35, 41–4
hierarchy 19, 21
hinge moment 153
Hoheisel, Tobias 96
Home Place, The (Friel) 128
Howard, Alan 3
humanist tradition 4, 14–15

iambic pentameter 53–4
Ibsen, Henrik
   Brand 182
   Doll's House, A 90, 148, 159
identification 6, 117, 158
Il Ritorno d'Ulisse in Patria (Monteverdi) 182
imagination/imagery 11, 37–9, 40, 42, 72
Importance of being Earnest (Wilde) 164
improvisation 155–69
   actor's view point 156
   aims 155–6
   blocking 145
   building a character 158–61
   building a company 156–8
   'gates' 160–1
   group sculpture 162–3
   large improvisations 168–9
   mask work 159
   memories 160–1
   moving in space 157
   as non-verbal exercises 156
   off the text 167–9
   relationships 161–7
   status games 164–5
   warm-up 157
   world of the play 161–7
in the round 90–2
inner obstacle 190
instinct 10–11, 96, 97, 183

journey of the play 30, 84–6
juxtaposition *see* apposition

Kane, Sarah 185
King Lear (Shakespeare)
    designing the journey of the play 84–5
    differing interpretations 118–19
    forest metaphor 29
    master and servant relationship 166
    singing in 107
    Tony Sher as Fool 195
Kingsley, Ben 198
Kiss Me Kate 213
Kushner, Tony 16

labelling scenes/sections of play 26, 66
language
    rehearsals 144, 152, 171–2, 191–2, 201
    seven elements used by Shakespeare 45–67
    world of the play 39–44
Lefton, Sue 159
life histories 166, 173–4
lighting design 49, 87, 88, 99, 101–2
Linbury Prize 70
line endings 56–9, 60, 124–5
Littlewood, Joan 203
live camera 89
living sculpture 162–3
Loach, Ken 16
logic 2, 19, 33, 112, 183–4
Love for Love (Congreve) 188
Love's Labour's Lost (Shakespeare) 61

Macbeth (Shakespeare)
    cuts 130–1
    designing the journey of the play 85–6
    Fears and Miseries scenes 204–5
    preview with Jonathan Pryce 217–18
    rhythm 55
    Verdi's opera 86
make-up 209
masks 159, 184
master and servant relationships 166–7
Measure for Measure (Shakespeare)
    forest metaphor 29
    paradigm of change 16
Mephisto 214
Merchant of Venice, The (Shakespeare) 103–4, 105–6
metaphor 29, 50–3, 123
metre 53–6, 124
micing 108
Midsummer Night's Dream, A (Shakespeare)
    beginning, middle and end exercise 26
    cast list 19–21, 32
    confusion 27
    crisis 27
    discussing character with actors during rehearsals 172–4
    entrances and exits 78–9, 87
    extreme actions 36
    family groups 20, 32, 33
    forests 29
    friendship groups 33
    improvisation exercises 164
    'in the round' exercise 91
    night time use 28
    obstacle 189
    rehearsals 142–3
    resolution 28, 29
    rhythm 53, 54–5
    word play 60–1
    world of the play 35, 39–41

mini runs 203
Mirren, Helen 10, 148
Mnouchkine, Ariane 16
model stage 74–5
moments of revelation 95
monosyllabic lines 64, 125
movement style 50
Much ado About Nothing
(Shakespeare) 188
music 103–8

names of cast 18, 20, 23
naturalistic plays, blocking 183, 184
Netrebko, Anna 86
night/nightmares 28–9
note-keeping 18, 19, 199, 200–1, 213–14

objectives 121–2, 173, 189
obstacle 189
off the book 191
on the book 150, 209–10
opening night 219–20
opera 5, 86, 96, 131, 182, 210
Oresteia (Aeschylus) 183
Ostrovsky, Alexander 3
outer obstacle 189

patriarchal society 33, 112
pauses 56, 124–5
Pericles (Shakespeare) 107
placing 144 *see also* blocking
Plantagenets, The 129
playhouses 14
playing card game 165
plumbing 46, 153, 171
political change 16
Postlethwaite, Pete 185
practice skirts 149
press night 219–20
previews 216–19

projection 88–9
Prologue 176–7
prompts 150
props 148, 159, 195
proscenium theatre 74–5
prose 42, 56
Pryce, Jonathan 217–18
psychological journey 29–30
public/private juxtaposition 48–9
pulse 53–6, 124

radio mics 108
read through 143, 152
reading the play 24–6
  out loud 72
recalls 114
Regietheater 5
regional accents 61, 62
rehearsals
  actions 173
  audibility issues 214
  basic aims 141–2
  beginning 142–4, 147–53, 171–4
  biographies of characters 166, 173–4
  blocked actors 193–6
  blocking 140, 144–5, 182–90, 192
  calls 149, 175–6, 191, 213
  costumes/garments 148–9, 159, 195, 209, 210–11
  curtain calls 215–16
  day one 147–53
  discussing characters with actors 172–4
  dress rehearsal 212–15
  feedback 204
  fight scenes 146, 210
  final day in rehearsal room 205–6
  first run through 197–202
  flexibility 142

furniture 148, 185–6
improvisation *see* improvisation
language 144, 152, 171–2, 192, 201
leading 142, 151
middle 144–6, 175–95
mini runs 203
nearly-at-the-end 146
non-actors in attendance 149–50
objectives 173
off the book 191
on the book 150, 209–10
plan 139, 142–6
prompts 150
props 148, 195
read through 143, 152
rehearsal room 148
run throughs 146, 197–204
second and third run throughs 203–4
second pass at scenes 190–6
set tasks 173
space needed 148, 149
stage management team 149–50
staggered run through 199
stakeholder contributions 215
storyboard 145
tank exercise 179–83
technical rehearsal (tech) 205–6, 207–12
traditional organization 140–1
wall of ideas 149
warm up 157, 178
weekly rep 141
relationships
family groups in cast 18, 20, 32–3
improvisation 161–7
resolution 27, 28–9, 30
revelation, moments of 95

reviews 219–20
rhyme 59–61
rhythm 53–6, 63, 124, 186
Richard III (Shakespeare) 186
Rickman, Alan 214
Romeo and Juliet (Shakespeare)
apposition 48
beginning, middle and end exercise 25
blocking 185–7
cast list 17–19, 32
chorus 176
confusion 27
crisis 27
cuts 135–6
extreme actions 36
family groups 18, 32, 33
friendship groups 33
imagery 38–9
improvisation exercises exploring relationships 162–3
large improvisations 168
metaphor 51–3
middle of rehearsals 178, 182–3
nightmare scenario 29
resolution 28, 29
staging 187
technical rehearsal 211
titles for sections of scenes 66
vocabulary 62–3
world of the play 35, 38–9
Roots (Wesker) 183, 184
Routledge, Patricia 105
Royal Shakespeare Company (RSC) 3, 4, 26, 109, 127, 172, 199, 217
run throughs 146, 197–203

safety issues 146, 210
scene changes 49, 94–5

weapons use 146, 210
weekly rep 141
Wesker, Arnold 128, 183, 184
West Side Story (Bernstein) 162
Who's Best curtain calls 216
Wilde, Oscar 164
Wilton, Penelope 160
Winter's Tale, The (Shakespeare)
    cuts 131–5

    large improvisations 169
    songs 105
women's roles 34, 111–12
word play 59–61
world of the play 17–24, 31–44, 72–3,
    161–7
writers
    cuts 128
    respecting 5

scene sections, labelling 26, 66
Seagull (Chekov) 107
Sekacz, Ilona 107
Sell, Colin 104
semicolons 58–9, 124
Serse (opera) 96
1789 (Mnouchkine) 16
shape 64–7, 130–7
Sher, Tony 195
shoes 101, 149
show and tell 97–8
situations 56, 158, 167–9, 185
skeleton of the play 83–4
small scene, big scene 48
songs and singing 105, 107
sonnet classes 172
sound designer 107–8
space of the play 75–6
speed run 219
stage management team 149–50
stage manager (SM) 149, 175, 210, 213
staging 49, 80, 87, 131, 178, 187
Stanislavski Method 6, 110, 117–25
    actions 118, 119–22, 173, 188–90, 191–2
    identification 6, 117
    objectives 121–2, 173, 189
status of characters 34, 164–5, 188
Stephens, Robert 85, 118–19
Stoppard, Tom 128
storyboard
    design process 97
    rehearsals 145
storytelling, art of 64–7
structure 64–7, 122–3
style of play 183–5
subject of play 19, 21, 24
Suchet, David 164
Swan Theatre 92–3

tank exercise 179–83
technical rehearsal (tech) 205–6, 207–12
texture 95–7
Theban plays (Sophocles) 159
three-step analysis of play 26–30
thrust stages 92–4
time line of play 130–6
titles for scenes/sections of play 26, 66
Titus Andronicus (Shakespeare) 185
tragedy 35
tragic axis 80–1
Travesties (Stoppard) 128
TV drama 16
Twelfth Night (Shakespeare)
    large improvisations 169
    songs 105
two-room theatre 75

Ultz, David 96
underscore 106

values of characters 165–6
video 88–9
virtual models 74
visualization 40–1
Vitruvian Man (Leonardo da Vinci) 75, 76
vocabulary 61–4, 125
von Trier, Lars 185
vowel sounds 64

wall of ideas
    design process 71–2
    rehearsals 149
walls, on stage 82–3
Ward, Anthony 71–2
warm up
    pre-performance 212
    rehearsal 157, 178